W9-CKE-961

THE LITTLE GIANT® BOOK OF
"True" Ghost Stories

Myers, Rau & Macklin
Illustrated by Jim Sharpe

THE
LITTLE GIANT®
SERIES

SCHOLASTIC INC.
New York Toronto London Auckland Sydney
Mexico City New Delhi Hong Kong Buenos Aires

No part of this publication may be reproduced in whole or in part, or stored in a retrieval system, or transmitted in any form or by any means, electronic, mechanical, photocopying, recording, or otherwise, without written permission of the publisher. For information regarding permission, write to Sterling Publishing Company, Inc., 387 Park Avenue South, New York, NY 10016.

ISBN 0-439-33995-2

The text of this book has been excerpted from
World's Most Bone-Chilling "True" Ghost Stories copyright © 1993
by Sterling Publishing Company, Inc.,
World's Most Terrifying "True" Ghost Stories copyright © 1995
by Arthur Myers, and reprinted from
World's Scariest "True" Ghost Stories copyright © 1994 by Margaret Rau.
Copyright © 1998 by Sterling Publishing Company, Inc.
Illustrations copyright © 1995 by Jim Sharpe.
All rights reserved.
Published by Scholastic Inc., 555 Broadway, New York, NY 10012,
by arrangement with Sterling Publishing Company, Inc.
SCHOLASTIC and associated logos are trademarks and/or
registered trademarks of Scholastic Inc.

12 11 10 9 8 7 6 5 4 3 2 1   1 2 3 4 5 6/0

Printed in the U.S.A.   01

First Scholastic printing, September 2001

Contents

1. GHOST AROUND THE HOUSE

The Haunted
Cleaning Lady

Ghosts abound on Nantucket Island, off the coast of
Massachusetts, as they do on many places near the water.
One theory is that the damp atmosphere makes it easier
for spirits to transfer their energy to us living people.
"Your mind is electrical," is the way one psychic puts it,
"and what is the best conductor of electricity? Water."

But although Margo Smith, as a native of Nantucket,

was no stranger to ghosts and stories of ghosts, when she took the job of cleaning Mrs. Deauville's house, it got to be just too much, although she stuck it out for quite a while. Her employer was away a lot, so during Margo's weekly cleaning chores she usually was alone in the house.

"On my first day at work," Margo recalls, "I brought my dog with me. He hopped out of the truck, ran up to the front door, and then wouldn't set foot inside."

He wouldn't go in the front door; he wouldn't go in the back door. She couldn't pull, push or carry him in. He had never done that at any other house. Margo thought to herself, "Oh no, here we go. There's something here."

The spirits—there seemed to be several—started playing with the phone. The first day, Margo was vacuuming when she heard the phone beeping as though someone had just taken it off the hook. She looked, and sure enough, the phone was off the hook.

Okay, she said to herself, I can deal with it. Then, as she was vacuuming, she heard the sound of a group of people, talking and laughing. She turned the vacuum off, and the house was dead silent. She turned the vacuum back on, and the party sounds started again, the high and low voices of women and men talking.

They were just warming up.

After a few weeks, the furniture began to move

around. If Margo was upstairs, she'd hear furniture dragged around downstairs. She'd gallop down the stairs and find that chairs and tables had been moved around.

These things happened only when she was alone in the house, when Mrs. Deauville and her family and guests were somewhere else. Perhaps Margo was a particularly psychic person, whom the spirits knew they could communicate with—and tease.

She never actually saw things being moved—only the results. "I was trying to straighten up and clean," she says, "and they were messing things up as fast as I could put them in order."

Margo never mentioned these happenings to Mrs. Deauville. She left it to her employer to bring up, if she wanted to, and she never did.

The spirits began to step up the pace. One day Margo was vacuuming under a bed, and something grabbed the front of the vacuum. It gave a little, as though something were holding on to it. When Margo pulled hard, the vacuum came loose from the hose and remained under the bed. After a considerable period of debate with herself, Margo worked up the courage to look under the bed. There was nothing there but the vacuum attachment. After another period of convincing herself there was nothing to be afraid of—hah!—Margo forced herself to reach under the bed and grab it.

12

Margo tried to reason with the ghosts. She'd open the front door and call, "Hello, I'm here. I'll be as quick as I can."

She didn't have much success. Furniture kept moving. Once, after a particularly long period of rumbling, she ran downstairs, to find all the living room chairs arranged in a circle.

Finally it got to be too much, even for Margo, the native Nantuckian. Pictures started coming down off the walls. Dishes clattered in the kitchen. A rug flew through the air and struck Margo in the back.

"I also got whacked," says Margo, "by some sofa pillows that zipped across the room on their own. Finally, a chair was thrown at me. It missed me, but that did it!"

Margo resigned.

A Very Bothersome Ghost

Some ghosts are rather intriguing to have around the house. They water the flowers, or bring in pleasant fragrances such as chocolate or baking bread, or something else they were associated with during life. Other ghosts, however, can be absolutely pesky—nobody you would want around, alive or dead.

An example of the pesky kind comes from Nollamara, a town in Western Australia.

Around 1970, Lee and Pat Decker and their baby son

moved into one of the oldest houses in town. Lee had gone into business for himself and had bought expensive equipment for his new factory.

The day after they moved in, they found a plain, sealed envelope in their letter box, containing ten dollars.

A few days later, Pat was dusting a window frame and a twenty-dollar bill fluttered down from the curtains. She spent the money.

When the couple went to bed one night, they found five ten-dollar bills strewn across the bed.

Lee refused to use this mysterious money. He said that, when he lived in Indonesia, he had heard of evil spirits who would leave money around to tempt people. The Deckers put the money in a cupboard. When they left the house for a while, they came back to find that the money had disappeared.

The ghost had some definitely annoying habits, however. One time all of Pat's clothes were removed from a closet and scattered across the floor of the bedroom. Sometimes articles of clothing disappeared. Sometimes they reappeared; some were gone for good.

The ghost would often take Lee's cigarettes, and sometimes pepper him with paper pellets while he was reading his newspaper. Once, though, when Lee complained, a new pack of cigarettes appeared on the kitchen table.

The ghost often stole food. Apples, pears, and cooked legs of chicken vanished. On the plus side, the ghost would occasionally wash dishes—although it rarely got them back on the right shelves.

One time the ghost stole a steak that Pat was preparing for Lee's lunch. She was so angry that she shouted at the ghost, and a few minutes later the steak reappeared on the plate.

The Deckers brought in clergymen to try to rid the place of the ghost, but they had little success.

The ghost's identity was not considered too much of a mystery in Nollamara. A man named Tom had formerly lived in the house, and had become very dejected after the death of his wife. He had committed suicide by hanging himself at the rear of the building.

The Deckers held a seance, and contacted a woman named Jean who had died in the house, presumably Tom's wife. But it didn't help. Soon after this, the Deckers moved out.

The house was demolished, leaving the newspapers in the area deprived of a subject that had fascinated their readers for many months.

A Wild and Crazy Lady Ghost

When Susan Strasberg, a well-known young actress, bought a house in Beverly Hills, California, she became a bit troubled. Her husband kept seeing a lady ghost around the house.

"Christopher was an actor and a bit eccentric," she would say jokingly. "But when he would talk to this lady and invite her to dance with him, it would give me the chills."

Susan became even more nervous when a physician friend, a quite level-headed young woman, visited her. After her first night, the friend related at breakfast that something had held her down in bed for a few minutes. She had the impression it was a woman.

Then Susan got a call from a friend who said he was sitting with a man who used to live in the house. The man wanted to know how was the lady.

'What lady?" asked Susan.

"The lady who haunts the house," her friend replied.

"I wish you hadn't told me this," Susan said.

She began to get really scared. "I had candles burning, and Bibles, and Jewish stars, and Buddhas," she says. "I wasn't taking any chances."

Susan had recently been in a film in Italy, where her stand-in had been a tiny young woman named Marina DeYorzo. They had become close friends.

"When this little girl and I walked down the street," Susan says, "the people thought she was a witch. They'd make a protective sign. They're very superstitious in Bari, the southern tip of Italy. Marina was almost an albino, and that made them think she was psychic, which to them would be a witch. She *was* very psychic, very open to other realities."

Soon after, Marina came to visit Susan in Beverly Hills. One day the two of them were doing yoga breathing, which can alter consciousness. Two male friends of Susan's husband were also in the room.

Suddenly, Susan relates, "Marina started to say in that strange accent—like Marlene Dietrich—'Wiolet, I see wiolet. How beautiful!' Then her tone changed to terror, and she cried, 'Oh, there's a woman! She's coming towards me! She's trying to possess me, she's trying to take over my body . . .'"

The men felt they had to get Marina out of the house, but she had a sudden ferocious strength. They could not hold her. She struck them over and over, bruising and scratching them.

Susan desperately phoned people for advice. She was sprinkling salt, saying the Lord's prayer, doing everything she had ever read or heard of.

"Marina had the strength of ten men," Susan says. "She was moaning and going through convulsions."

They finally managed to drag her out the front door. The instant she crossed the threshold, she stopped struggling and said, "What are you holding me for? Put me down!"

When they told her what had happened, she wanted to go back into the house. She wasn't going to let the ghost intimidate her.

Susan vetoed that idea. She packed suitcases and they moved to a hotel until Marina left.

Susan brought in psychics, priests, Indian mystics to try to clear the house, but she doesn't believe they were successful.

Her husband would catch glimpses of the ghost, and a guest reported one morning that something had held her down in bed momentarily.

"I never found out who the ghost was," Susan says.

Something Black and Cold

It started with little things, strange incidents that were sometimes inconvenient, sometimes almost amusing. But then the heavy trouble began, and the terror.

In the early 1970s, two sisters, Lois Dean and

Diantha Summer, moved their families into two old houses in the middle of Rawlins, Wyoming, a small city in the Rocky Mountains. Lois and her husband and their six children moved into the big house. Diantha and her two sons took the carriage house right behind.

Very soon, strange things started happening in the big house.

• Lights kept turning on and off. At first, the adults thought it was just the kids playing around. But they soon found that lights seemed to be going on or off by themselves, when no one was around. Lois and her husband had the big house rewired, but it kept happening.

• When the children were playing games, they would leave the room for a moment and come back to find pieces missing.

• An older daughter found the colors of her makeup often ran together. At first, she thought the younger children were doing it, but she padlocked her bedroom and it kept happening.

• The family dog wagged his tail as though at an invisible guest, and his eyes followed something across the room.

• Sometimes in the big house the bathroom cabinet would be found completely empty. Toothbrushes, combs and medicines would be gone, to be found later in odd places. Again, Lois thought it was the children, but it happened when they were at school and she was alone in the house.

Then things began to get rough.

A boyfriend of one of the girls was playfully climbing through a window. Something unseen picked him up and threw him inside, up against the wall. That was the end of that boyfriend. He never came back for another visit.

Not long afterward, one of the younger boys said he thought he had seen something in the garage. Mike, Diantha's 14-year-old son, decided to take a look. He started out the back door of the big house and suddenly felt two hands grab him and throw him through the air, back into the kitchen against the refrigerator. He had red marks on his chest as though something had scratched him.

Lois was infuriated. She began yelling, "I don't care who you are, I'm not putting up with you coming into my house and hurting kids!"

So angry that she was momentarily unafraid, she dashed out into the garage. There she saw a black shape.

"It was big and billowy," she says, "and it was dressed like a woman in something black and long."

It came toward her smoothly, as though it were on wheels.

"Something black and cold started coming out of it, like ribbons," she recalls. "It started wrapping me in those strands. I could feel their coldness. I could not move."

Then she felt her sister, who saw the shape too, grab her from behind and jerk her away from the thing and back to the big house.

The sisters sat up all night, praying as hard as they could. The prayers may have had a good effect, for they never saw the thing again.

They took to calling that incident "the main event." Afterward, they felt the atmosphere to be a little less oppressive. However, everyone had a sense that the place was still not quite right, and before long both families moved out.

What on earth was happening there? Lois feels she got a strong clue when she talked with an aged aunt who had lived in the neighborhood in the early 1900s.

"She told me," Lois says, "that there had been a graveyard on that property, and the bodies were dug up and moved to a larger cemetery somewhere else in town. But there was talk that two bodies had been left behind."

Was that the answer? Throughout the world there have been many, many reports of cemeteries dug up and moved. And if there are bodies left behind, the spirits who once resided in them are thought to become restless and make their presence known to those of us who are still alive.

2. HAUNTED PLACES

The Haunted Museum

One of the favorite public haunted places in Toronto, Canada, is a museum called the Mackenzie House, but the people who work there don't seem to enjoy it as much as casual visitors do. In fact, the people who take care of the place often find it pretty scary.

The house was once the home of William Mackenzie, who was at one time the mayor of Toronto, but he made so many enemies that for a time he had to flee Canada and take refuge in the United States.

Now that he is safely dead, he seems to have returned to his Toronto home. Some caretakers have seen him.

One, a Mrs. Edmunds, tells of seeing the apparition of a small, bald man in an old-fashioned frock coat. This certainly sounds like Mackenzie, although in life he usually wore a red wig. Perhaps he has mislaid it in the next world. Or maybe he has become less vain about his appearance.

Mackenzie published a small newspaper, and the press on which he printed it is still in the cellar. It is kept locked, but many staff members swear they have heard rumbling below that sounds suspiciously like an old-time printing press going full tilt.

Another ghost, more belligerent toward the living than Mackenzie, is that of a woman. Mrs. Edmunds has had her problems with this one. She tells of awakening at night to see a woman with dark brown hair and a narrow face, leaning over and staring at her intently. A few months later, Mrs. Edmunds awoke again to see the ghostly woman. This time the ghost struck her in the face, giving her a black eye.

The Edmunds children keep seeing the ghost of a

woman in the bathroom, a ghost that disappears on being sighted. Plants in the house are often watered mysteriously—and sometimes carelessly, for the curtains are splashed with mud.

It's not on record exactly how long the Edmunds put up with these shenanigans before moving out. However, it *is* on record that other caretakers have also had their troubles. Many have reported that the toilets flushed by themselves, and that water taps turned on when there was no one—alive—around to do this.

A caretaker named Mrs. McCleary says she often feels as though a ghost is putting its arms around her. However, since the spirit remains invisible, it's anyone's guess whether it is Mackenzie or the lady ghost.

Whenever renovation work is done at the house, workmen come up with a whole new batch of anecdotes about the place. Often objects such as sawhorses, ropes and drop sheets are found in the morning to have been moved around, even though the building had been locked all night. And one workman, Murdo MacDonald, gained fame when he was first into the house one morning and found a hangman's noose over a stairway.

It's no wonder that the Mackenzie House is one of the favorite stops on Halloween ghost tours in Toronto.

A Very Firm Disbeliever

A wealthy young couple had built a large, elaborate house near Gulfport in Mississippi. Their teenage daughter committed suicide there. The parents were, of course, extremely sorrowful. But only a few days later, they fled the house taking a minimum of clothing, never to return.

Their hasty departure did not suggest sorrow as

much as it did extreme fear. Rumors quickly spread that the house was now haunted.

Fran Franklin, now a professor of journalism at the University of Arkansas, was nine years old at the time. She had a favorite aunt, Harriet Gibbons, who was an unusual person. Tiny—only four feet tall—she was the editor of a daily newspaper in Mississippi, and she had very definite opinions. She knew the young couple, and ridiculed their flight as pure superstition.

"There is no such thing as a ghost," Harriet often said.

She said she planned to stay in the house overnight to prove there was nothing to be frightened of. Fran asked if she could go along, and her aunt agreed.

So one night, the two let themselves into the house with a key that Harriet had gotten from friends. They set two chairs in the front hallway and sat down to wait for something to happen. Around midnight, something happened.

Upstairs, they heard a door close. Then they heard what sounded like footsteps coming down the hall. Fran looked at the top of the wide staircase, expecting to see a ghostly figure, but she saw nothing. However, she could *hear* the footsteps coming down the stairs! As they reached the bottom of the stairs, Fran could see a depression in the carpet. When the footsteps reached the marble floor, they clicked across the foyer. They clicked down the hall to a set of double doors that opened into a music room. The doors opened.

Fran was terrified. She looked at her little aunt for a cue. Harriet sat unmoving, her face expressionless.

The footsteps continued across the floor of the music room, stopping at a piano that was visible from the foyer. As Fran and Harriet watched, the piano stool came back. The top covering the piano keys was raised, revealing the keyboard. A short concert of three pieces by Chopin came from the piano.

Then the music stopped. The cover of the keyboard came back down. The piano stool moved back to its original position.

The sound of steps came out of the room. The double doors closed. The steps tapped back across the marble foyer to the foot of the stairs. There they hesitated, as though the unseen performer was momentarily observing her audience of two. Then the footsteps went back up the stairs, and back down the upstairs hall. Fran and her aunt heard a door upstairs close.

Aunt Harriet turned to Fran. "It's time to go now," she said.

As they were driving back to their motel, Fran got up the courage to ask Aunt Harriet what she thought of all this.

"There is no such thing as a ghost," Aunt Harriet replied.

The Tale of a Thief

Charlie Sennett was an easygoing cowpoke, a good man to have along on a roundup or back in the bunkhouse. For he was an amusing fellow, always good for a story or a comradely laugh. He told most of his tales with a chuckle and a wink.

But there was one story he rarely told. And when he did tell it, he never laughed or winked. He stared intently into the fire as though he saw his fate there, and didn't like it one bit. People wondered why Charlie told the story at all. Some said he did it to humble himself, to make amends for something of which he was very much ashamed.

Charlie was born in Wyoming and lived and punched cattle there all his life. He had this experience, the most frightening of his life, when he was a young man of 19, in the year 1950.

The story involved a sacred Native American tradition. Charlie was well aware of what he was doing, for he was part Native American himself. And he couldn't excuse himself because he was young at the time. Native American children learn this custom very early in life.

The tradition is that a grave should never, never be disturbed.

Charlie knew of a kinsman who had been buried in a cave in an out-of-the-way canyon in a desolate area called Dinwoodie. The man, whose Native American name was Low Thunder, had been wealthy. He had owned much land and many cattle. Around his grave had been reverently placed his most prized possessions, for many Native Americans believed that a person's spirit could use these things in the next life. Charlie especially admired a splendid saddle that had been left beside the grave, so that Low Thunder could ride it in the Happy Hunting Grounds.

Charlie, a poor young man, had an old saddle so worn it was coming apart. He had just taken a new job at a ranch, and he hated to show up with this shabby saddle. He could not get his mind off the magnificent saddle at the grave of Low Thunder. After all, Charlie told himself, he had as much white blood as Native American. Why should he let himself be bound by superstition?

One day, when he found himself in the vicinity of the canyon, he made up his mind. He reined his horse into the canyon and climbed to the cave. He hesitated as he reached its mouth, telling himself it was not Low Thunder he was afraid of, but the rattlesnakes that swarmed in such caves. These live creatures, poisonous though they were, seemed less fearsome to him than an angry spirit. Encouraged, he plunged into the cave and quickly found the grave. There was the saddle, as beautiful as it had been when first placed there. He scooped it into his arms and ran. He pulled his old saddle off his horse, threw it over a cliff, put the saddle of Low Thunder on the horse and galloped away.

Far from the canyon, Charlie slowed his horse to a trot. Joy surged through him. No need to feel guilty, he told himself. How can you steal from the dead?

Suddenly he felt a thud behind him, as though someone had landed in the saddle! He heard a ghastly whisper in his ear. "Take back that saddle!" it hissed.

Charlie broke out in a cold sweat. He whipped his horse into a gallop, as though he could outrun whatever was clinging to him—as though he could leave that whisper behind.

But now the voice did not whisper. It roared, "Take back that saddle!" It bellowed, "Take back that saddle!"

His horse stumbled. It veered as though trying to turn. It twisted its head, eyes wide and huge. It was terrified. For animals are even more aware of spirits than humans are.

Charlie gave up. He whirled the horse around and sped back to the canyon. Uncinching the saddle, he raced into the cave and dropped it beside the grave. Then he leaped onto his frightened horse and rode off as though his life depended on it.

Miles away, he came to the lonely ranch of a friend. The man's wife is still alive, and she tells of Charlie's arrival that day. "He was riding bareback," she relates, "and he asked if he could borrow a saddle. I tried to give him dinner, but he broke down. He couldn't stop crying. He said he had stolen a saddle from a kinsman's grave. 'But I took it back,' he sobbed over and over, 'I took it back, I took it back . . .'"

A Very Strange Telephone Call

Mammoth Cave National Park, in Kentucky, contains perhaps the most famous collection of caves in the world. According to many people who work there as guides, or who are among the 2,000,000 tourists who visit the caves each year, there are ghosts in those caverns.

The most convincing witnesses might well be members of the Cave Research Foundation, which numbers some 650 scientists who investigate caves all over the United States. Their headquarters are at Mammoth

Park. Most CRF members are professors at universities, not the sort of people who would make up stories about ghostly experiences. But things happen. As one CRF member put it:

"We're a bunch of hard-nosed people. Most of us who have had these experiences are not believers in ghosts, ordinarily. We just describe the facts and let others decide."

Two CRF members who had a chilling experience are Dr. Will White, a professor of geochemistry at Pennsylvania State University, and Dr. George Deike, a government scientist. They were investigating Crystal Cave, which is no longer open to the public. However, it had once been open to tourists, and there was an old army field telephone down in the cave.

"I guess they used it," White says, "to let the guides know some people were coming, tell them to wake up."

On this day, White and Deike, on their way through the cave to do some geological exploration, were walking by this ancient, broken-down phone—when suddenly, it rang!

The two scientists were too startled, perhaps too fearful, to stop. They kept walking down the passageway.

White says, "When we got about 200 feet farther on, the phone rang again! We looked at each other for a moment, then we ran back. I picked up the old phone and answered. It was one of those old-fashioned army phones with a sort of butterfly switch on it.

"What I heard sounded like a phone sounds when it's off the hook and there are people in the room. You hear the sounds of voices, but you can't tell what they are saying. I said hello, or something like that. And on the other end there's a startled gasp. And that was all. No one responded. The line was now dead."

Astonished, the two scientists noticed that the phone was attached to a rusty, twisted phone line. They traced it back to the mouth of the cave, and out to a weathered shack that had once been a ticket office. But the phone line ended there. It was attached to nothing!

Had Dr. White heard the sounds of another world?

3. STRANGE!

The Dog Who Was Scared to Death by a Ghost

They called him Chief, because he had once been owned by the police.

He belonged to the Iannucci family, who owned a restaurant in Glen Mills, Pennsylvania. The building had been an old farmhouse, built 250 years before, and they were rebuilding the old place.

As often happens when buildings are changed, it stirs up ghosts. They don't like changes. There was one especially frightening spirit. It threw vases and flashed lights off and on. Sometimes it appeared as a greyish form hovering over people in bed. But the living being that was most frightened by this ghost was Chief.

Jerry Iannucci had bought the dog from the police department in nearby Upper Darby. Chief's days were numbered, Jerry had heard, because Chief was so vicious and aggressive that he could not be controlled. The police were going to have to, as they put it, "terminate" him. Jerry figured that Chief would be perfect to have around the house to guard it while it was being renovated.

However, Jerry says, "The dog turned into a wimp as soon as he got here. There was something here that would cause him to creep around and cower in the corners."

One of the Iannucci sons, Rick, was living in the building, and Chief would constantly stay close by him. One night, however, Rick was away and the dog had to stay in the building by himself. Another son, Rob, arrived in the morning to do some work and found Chief obviously terrified.

"That dog was always freaked out here, from the moment we got him," Rob says. "He would completely shy away from certain areas of the building, and he especially stayed away from the third floor."

The third floor, called the "loft," was being restored as living quarters for some of the family.

When Rob arrived that morning, the dog followed him around, staying as close as possible. "He was really palling around with me," Rob says. "After a while I had to go up to the loft. I could see he didn't want to go up there, but he didn't want to be alone, so he finally followed me up the stairs. When we got up there, I started working on a bookcase at one end of a long room.

"The dog was acting very strange. He would freeze, just stand stiffly and stare. You would think that somebody else was in the room. Then the dog started flinching. It was as though somebody was doing something to him. It was like something was standing next to him and threatening to hit him with a stick, or poking him. The dog started howling, and looking around wildly. He saw an open window and just dove through it, three stories above the ground. He was killed, of course."

"And," says Jerry Iannucci, "this was a dog who was so fierce that the police were going to shoot it."

The Disembodied Arm

Major MacGregor was a brave man. He had faced shot and shell and enemy soldiers in battle. But now he was terrified. This was something very different!

It was a night in 1871, and he was lying in bed in the elegant house of a cousin in Dublin, Ireland. He had been visiting his cousin when her husband became ill, and MacGregor had sat up with him several nights. But now the man seemed better, and MacGregor went to bed, asking a servant to call him if his host took a turn for the worse.

MacGregor, exhausted, fell asleep immediately. An hour later, he felt a push on his shoulder. He started up, thinking it was the servant.

"Is anything wrong?" he asked in the darkened room.

He got no answer, only another push.

The major got exceedingly annoyed. "Speak, man," he bellowed, "and tell me if anything is wrong!"

He still got no reply, but he had a feeling he was going to get another push. He twisted around in bed, reached out and grasped what seemed to be a human hand. It was warm and soft, a woman's hand.

"Who are you?" he demanded, but got no answer.

He tried to pull the hand towards him, but the owner of the hand seemed quite strong, and he was unable to.

Thoroughly irritated, MacGregor exclaimed, "I am determined to find out who you are!"

He held the hand tightly in his right hand, and with his left began to feel the wrist and arm. They seemed to be clothed in a tight-fitting sleeve, with a linen cuff.

When he got to the elbow, there was nothing more! All trace of the rest of the arm had disappeared! MacGregor was so astonished that he let go of the hand.

The next morning, he told of his strange experience. His hostess took his tale calmly.

His cousin said, "Oh, that was old Aunt Betty. She lived in the upper part of the house and died many years ago."

44

Aunt Betty had been a very nice person, she assured him, so there was nothing to worry about.

But when MacGregor talked with the servants, they were not so encouraging. Sometimes, they said, Aunt Betty's arm pulled the bedclothes off. One lady had received a slap in the face from an invisible hand.

MacGregor's cousin insisted that Aunt Betty would never think of hurting anyone. Maybe so, MacGregor reflected silently, but she just might scare you to death.

The Pilot Who Saw a Dread Future

Throughout history there has been evidence that at times some people have caught glimpses of the future. Often these pictures of approaching events come in dreams. But they are also seen by people who are fully awake. Take the experience of George Potter, a Royal Air Force pilot during World War II.

Wing Commander Potter was stationed at a base called RAF Shallufa in Egypt. From this base, bombing planes flew out over the Mediterranean Sea to plant torpedoes and mines in the paths of ships carrying supplies to the North African desert forces of the German General Erwin Rommel. This was a crucial period of the war, the first time the Allied armies were winning. They were pushing back the forces of the Germans' most successful general, known as the Desert Fox.

The airmen's missions were extremely dangerous. Between bombing runs there was much nervous gaiety as they tried to forget the peril of their lives. They ate, drank, sang and laughed as though they were schoolboys, which they had been not long before.

One evening, Commander Potter entered the Officers' Mess with a friend, Flying Officer Reg Lamb. At a nearby table, a group of flyers were celebrating something— perhaps that they were still alive. One of them was a wing commander whom Potter refers to as Roy.

After a few moments, Potter heard a loud burst of laughter from the table, and glanced over that way. As he has described it:

"I turned and saw the head and shoulders of Roy moving ever so slowly in a background of blue-blackness. His lips were drawn back from his teeth in a dreadful grin. He had no eyes in his eye sockets. The flesh of his face was blotched in greenish, purplish shadows."

A few seconds later, Potter felt Reg Lamb tugging at his sleeve. "What's the matter?" Lamb asked. "You've gone white as a sheet. You look as if you've seen a ghost!"

"I *have* seen a ghost," Potter replied. "Roy over there has the mark of death on him."

Lamb looked over at the table of joking officers, but could see nothing unusual.

That night Roy was shot down. He and his crew were seen clambering into a life raft, but the air-sea rescue planes were unable to find them. The flyers were never heard from again.

"I then knew what I had seen," Potter relates. "The blue-black background was the sea at night, and Roy was floating in it, dead, with his head and shoulders held up by his life jacket."

4. MESSAGES FROM GHOSTS

A Call from Uncle Andy

The idea of phone calls from the dead may seem outlandish, but while they don't exactly clutter up the phone lines, they are not as uncommon as one might think. Many people have received calls that seem to come from another world.

Once such phone call was experienced by Ida Lupino, who was a movie star during the middle of the 20th century. Although Ida became famous in Hollywood, she had been born and brought up in England, a member of a theatrical family that went back for generations. Her father and mother, Stanley and Connie Lupino, were well-known performers in the English variety theater. When Ida was nine, they were living in London at her grandmother's house.

One night, Ida had a disturbing dream about a man she called Uncle Andy, a friend of her parents. She woke up, and went downstairs to tell her grandmother, who was preparing a late supper for Stanley and Connie. While Ida was telling her grandmother about her dream, the phone rang. Her grandmother asked Ida to answer it.

"I went to the phone," Ida relates, "took it off the hook and heard a voice on the line. But it was so faint I could scarcely understand the words. Finally, the voice became stronger and I could understand the message, repeated monotonously several times: 'I must talk to Stanley. It is terribly important.'"

The little girl recognized the voice as that of Uncle Andy. She said her father wasn't home yet. But the voice kept saying the same thing over and over. Ida called her grandmother to the phone. She heard her grandmother say, "Andy, are you *ill*? I'll ask Stanley to call you the moment he comes in."

Then the call was cut off. Ida's grandmother protested angrily to the operator, who insisted there had not been a call on the line in the past hour.

Stanley and Connie returned a half hour later and Ida told them that Uncle Andy had called. They looked very upset, and tried to send her to bed.

But her grandmother backed her up. "She's not mistaken, Stanley," she said. "I heard Andy too. I think you had better call him. He sounded as though he were ill."

Ida says she has never forgotten how shaken her father's voice sounded when he replied:

"Mom," he said, "Andy is dead. He hanged himself three days ago."

Help from a Ghost

Donald Campbell was a famous Australian race driver. He was the son of another famed driver, Sir Malcolm Campbell.

After his father's death, Donald went on to establish his own fame. But for a long time, he missed the elder Campbell's advice and encouragement.

In 1964, he was driving a racing car on Lake Eyre, a dry salt lake in Australia. He was seeking a new world speed record. In one of the first of two mile runs, he had almost crashed. He still had the other run to go.

The salt track was breaking up, and he knew that the second run would be even more difficult and dangerous than the first. His crew was changing the car's tires. Sitting in his cockpit, Donald wondered if this would be a disastrous run, if he were experiencing the last few minutes of his life.

As the child of a world-famous race driver, Donald was very much aware of the extreme danger of the sport. Going through his mind at this time was an experience his father had had many years before while trying for a world speed record. A wheel had caught fire, and Sir Malcolm had narrowly escaped being killed. Donald had often wondered how his father had felt in the face of imminent death.

Now, waiting for his second and final run, this memory was uppermost in his mind.

One of the crew, Ken Norris, who was also one of the designers of the car, happened to look through the windshield and he noticed that Campbell was staring upwards intently. The driver's face had been filled with tension. Norris had a powerful sense of his driver's fear. But then Campbell's expression relaxed. He appeared now to be calm.

He then drove out and made a successful run.

Later, Campbell told his friend:

"It was the most incredible thing I've ever experienced. On the first run, I nearly killed myself. I knew the second run would be worse. I saw no hope at all.

"Suddenly I looked up and saw my father, just as clearly as I'm seeing you now. He was looking at me, smiling. Then he said, 'Well, boy, now you know how I felt that time in Utah when a wheel caught fire. But don't worry, it will be all right.'

"And he faded away. And indeed, it *was* all right."

The Ghost of a Deformed Monk

Maurice Maeterlinck was a famous playwright who won the Nobel Prize for literature in 1911. At the time, he was living in France, in a centuries-old building called St. Wandrille Abbey, once inhabited by priests and monks. It had been converted into a private dwelling. It was also reputed to be haunted. This did not bother Maeterlinck, for he was fascinated by ghosts, often referring to them in his works. However, he had never had a ghostly experience in the old abbey, until . . .

A number of guests were visiting, including the famous Russian actor/director Constantin Stanislavsky. An American woman was staying in another part of the house. In the middle of the night, the occupants were awakened by her screams. As the others gathered, she stammered that she had seen the apparition of a deformed monk.

Maeterlinck was not one to return to bed and let it go at that. Nor were his guests. They immediately made an attempt to communicate with the ghost through table tipping. And they were successful. The table rapped out a message from the spirit who claimed to be a monk named Bertrand.

"Oh save me, save me!" the table tapped out. There was a desperate tone to the message.

The listeners spread out through the building, looking for evidence. Stanislavsky found a plaque on which was inscribed in Latin:

"Bertrand: pax vobiscum: AD 1693."

Or, "Peace be with you."

Maeterlinck had heard there was a secret room in the abbey, and the company searched the place, looking for hiding places. Eventually, Maeterlinck found a hollow panel and pushed it open.

In a small compartment, they found the bones of a man who had been terribly deformed in life, and who had apparently died there, where he had been walled in.

A Terrifying Visitor

The two young military officers sat in a small apartment, completely unaware of the unusual visitor they were about to have.

They were drinking tea, relaxing from their duties. The apartment was part of a British Army barracks in Sydney, Nova Scotia. It was the afternoon of October 15,

1785. They were Lieutenant George Wynyard and Captain John Sherbrooke.

Suddenly Sherbrooke looked up and gasped. Wynyard followed his friend's gaze, and dropped the cup from which he had been sipping.

For the two officers saw a young man, about 20, standing at the door. The youth looked very ill. He was dressed in lightweight clothing, despite the cold Nova Scotia weather.

The young man entered the room and walked by the two seated men. Sherbrooke later described the figure as having "the appearance of a corpse." The young man glanced sadly at Wynyard and then, as the officers watched, spellbound, went through the doorway into Wynyard's bedroom.

Wynyard leaped to his feet. "Great heavens," he cried, "that's my brother!"

They rushed into the bedroom, but no one was there.

Communications were slow in those days. It was months later when Wynyard received a letter from India, where his favorite brother, John, had been serving in the British Army. The letter brought the news that John had died—the previous October.

Monkeys in the Closet

Beatrice Straight, a prize-winning stage and film actress, lived in New York City, but often spent weekends at a house that had belonged to her late parents, in Old Westbury, Long Island.

It was a spooky old place, with many Oriental ornaments that had been collected by her father, Willard Straight. He had been a U.S. consul in Manchuria, a region of China. He had also created a Chinese garden on the little estate.

Beatrice's thoughts were running to ghosts at this time, for she had recently appeared on Broadway in a scary play called *The Innocents*. It was based on "Turn of the Screw," a famous ghost story by the writer Henry James. The story had been adapted for the stage by playwright William Archibald, who was also very interested in ghosts.

One weekend, Beatrice and her husband, Peter Cookson, brought a group of friends out from New York City, including William Archibald, to spend a country weekend. That evening, Archibald suggested that they do some table tipping. Beatrice recalls:

"Bill told us what to do, that the table would tip and tap out letters on the floor. For example, one tap equalled an A, five taps meant E, and so on through the alphabet. We went up to a bedroom my father had used and sat around a small table with our hands on top, and it suddenly started to go like mad, tipping and all.

"It said it was a spirit from the Gobi Desert. Sometimes the table would raise up above our heads, shaking, and then crash. We broke two tables that way.

But before the second table broke, it spelled out:

MONKEYS IN THE CLOSET.

"I went to the closet in the room that I'd never looked in before. It was full of books that had been put there way back when. The table kept spelling out, MONKEYS IN THE CLOSET. I started pulling books out, and there at the back of the closet was an ivory statue with twelve monkeys on it. It was an ivory tree, and the monkeys were going up the tree."

By this time, everybody was getting pretty nervous. So when the table tapped out: BURY ME IN THE GARDEN, they thought that was a very good idea. They were eager to get the statue out of the house and out of sight. So the whole group took it out and buried it in the Chinese garden.

Half an hour later, Archibald went to his bedroom and came out to say somebody must be kidding him. For on his pillow he had found one of the little ivory monkeys. But then everybody realized that the monkeys were not detachable. The statue was a solid block of ivory.

The next morning, they found another ivory monkey on the steps of the front door.

When *The Innocents* had first been produced, famous psychic Eileen Garrett had been engaged as a consultant. Beatrice now went to her and told her what had happened.

"She said to go back and dig up the statue," Beatrice relates. "She said don't do these things unless you're with somebody who really knows what it is all about, that there are spirits who are naughty and can cause trouble."

The next weekend, Beatrice and her husband went to the Chinese garden to dig up the statue. And there was no statue there!

5. POLTERGEISTS ?
OR
SOMETHING
ELSE?

When Is a Ghost Not a Ghost?

Hundreds of curious, fearful people surrounded the little house in Bridgeport, Connecticut. Some tried to burn it down, convinced it harbored a witch. Others threw garlic, an ancient protection against witches, onto the front steps. For very strange things were happening in this house.

It was occupied by Gerald Goodin; his wife, Laura;

and their adopted daughter, Marcia, 11. They often heard tapping, banging sounds. Lights would go on and off. So did the TV. This was just a warm-up for terror.

Early one morning, Gerald Goodin noticed that a large refrigerator had turned from its usual position. The kitchen table began to flip up and down. Chairs fell over.

He heard a crash from his wife's bedroom. A religious picture had fallen off the wall. An even louder crash came from Marcia's room. Her bureau had fallen over. Wearing only nightclothes, the Goodins fled out into the street.

A policeman lived nearby, and he went into the house, but left when the refrigerator began teetering back and forth.

All sorts of explanations were offered—an earthquake, an underground stream, the house settling. Police came to the house to guard the Goodins. Experts on hauntings flooded in from all over the country.

Among them was a Connecticut man named Boyce Batey. He talked with many witnesses, and saw and heard many strange things himself. The turning point in his investigation came on New Year's Day, 1975, when he was sitting in the Goodins' kitchen.

A stereo set moved, and a table went up and down with a bang. Acting on a suspicion, he ran into Marcia's bedroom. The girl was lying on the bed, face down.

"That didn't seem right to me," Batey says. "When a loud sound is heard, the tendency is to go towards it."

A picture in the bedroom fell from the wall, scattering glass across the floor. Marcia still lay motionless.

Batey and other investigators began to develop a theory: the commotions were not being caused by a ghost or demon, they were being caused by Marcia.

It is becoming well known that some people can cause things to move without touching them. They can cause raps and bangs without hitting anything. This is called "parakinesis."

It happens particularly when people are emotionally disturbed. Often these people are teenagers or slightly younger, for this is often a difficult time of life. And Marcia had more than her share of problems. The Goodins had had a young son who had died. They had adopted Marcia, a Native American Iroquois from a reservation in Canada, in an effort to lessen their grief.

They were so protective of Marcia that she had almost no outside life. Batey says, "This girl was a very normal child. She was intelligent, artistic, gentle, sweet."

But she had almost no social contacts. Mrs. Goodin walked her to school and back. Some children taunted her about her Native American heritage. One kicked her in the back so severely that she was forced to stay home for weeks. It was when she was almost healed and was about to be sent back to her scary school life that the heavy poltergeist activity—things moving around—began.

Batey felt that initially it was Marcia's way of expressing anger at her parents and the world. Afterwards, she wanted to keep the excitement going and the company coming. The police in the house made a fuss over her. Her little game had brought social life into the house.

Batey recalls: "One time, Marcia and a policeman were playing a game of checkers, and he won. Within three minutes, a bedroom bureau fell over, and a TV set fell onto the floor. Marcia had been disappointed by her defeat, but was too gentle to express it in an ordinary way."

So it would seem that not all poltergeists come from another world. Some come from ordinarily harmless people who are very much part of this one.

A Fatal Apparition

When Arthur Koestler, a well-known writer, was a young man he was invited to a house in the Austrian Alps by a wealthy, very attractive woman named Maria Kloepfer, the widow of a German movie star. Soon after he arrived, she asked him if he believed in ghosts. He passed the question off with a joke. However, his hostess said casually that if he heard knocking on the walls at night to ignore it. She was plagued with poltergeists (noisy ghosts), she explained, but they were harmless.

He was soon subjected to more than mere noise. As they were sitting at lunch the next day, a large picture that hung on the wall behind Maria came crashing down. Koestler inspected the picture carefully and noted that the wire that held it up had not broken, and the two hooks to which the wire had been fastened remained solidly in the wall. He was mystified, but even more so by the fact that his hostess had not moved a muscle. This sort of thing was apparently nothing new to her.

When her aging maid came in and asked what had happened, Maria answered simply, "The haunting."

In a nearby village, Koestler heard vague murmurs about apparitions at his hostess's house, but he considered himself a rational person and paid no attention.

One afternoon, he and Maria went walking in the woods. Her small dog, Ricky, ran along ahead. Koestler described what happened:

"Suddenly Ricky stopped, rooted to the mossy ground, and gave out a growl which then changed into a plaintive, long-drawn howl. Maria also stopped and grabbed my arm. Her face had changed color, pale beneath her sunburnt skin. Her lips drew back and the braces on her teeth were visible. The wailing dog's hair was actually bristling. I felt suspended between horror and the giggles."

Maria turned and ran back towards the house, the dog by her side. "Now and then," Koestler wrote, "he licked her hand as if to comfort her."

Later she told Koestler, "Ricky saw my uncle approaching us. He sometimes sees him first and warns me."

She said it was the apparition of a dead uncle whom she had feared and hated, who had mistreated her as a small child. He had become insane, and had died when she was three.

Recently, she had begun seeing his ghost. She said that the apparition in the woods had appeared as a triple image—one coming towards her from the front and two simultaneously approaching from left and right.

Koestler left soon afterwards. A few weeks later, he heard that she had died in an institution. The elderly maid told Koestler that the apparition of the uncle had appeared on the veranda, and her mistress had had an epileptic seizure, from which she never recovered.

Pebbles from Heaven

Gilbert Smith and his wife and children lived in a small cottage in Western Australia, a dwelling that occupied the bewildered attention of millions of Australians for some weeks in 1955.

The mystery was pebbles. Pebbles raining from "nowhere."

This was farming country, and the Smiths, who were part Aboriginal, were engaged in growing flax. The land was owned by Bill Hack.

When pebbles began to fall on the Smith house, they thought it might be a joke. Mr. Smith went to his employer, Mr. Hack, to see if he might be able to deal with the situation. Hack did not take the matter seriously, but when he pulled up to the Smiths' house a pebble hit the roof of his car and bounced off, striking him on the shoulder. This, incidentally, was the only record of a person being struck by a pebble, though thousands of them fell.

During the time that Hack was in the house that day, many pebbles fell on the roof. Even more baffling, several landed on the living room floor, although there were no holes in the roof!

Word spread, and soon friends and neighbors gathered to surround the house with spotlights. They could see the pebbles falling on the roof and onto the surrounding ground, where they were standing. No member of the search party was ever struck.

Some nights the groups brought shotguns and fired them into the air. They also brought dogs, who seemed as mystified as the people.

The newspapers sent reporters, who saw stones varying in size from a match-head to a hen's egg. They fell on the cars and on the floor and the furniture inside the Smith house. Some of the stones were warm or hot, others were not.

Bill Hack was concerned about the safety of the Smith family, so he drove 90 miles to the town of Mt. Barker and returned with a native witch doctor, Sammy Miller.

74

Miller suggested that the disturbance was being caused by the spirit of Mrs. Smith's father, who at the time was dangerously ill in a hospital. He had been taken ill while working near the Smiths' home. Mrs. Smith resisted this idea, but was startled when Miller went, without any direction from anyone, to a post hole not far away from where her father had been working when he had a heart attack. Miller said that at that moment the elderly man's spirit had left him.

The mystic said that when an Aborigine was close to death his spirit left him but it would linger about until the person died or recovered. He said there was no need for fear, that the spirit was a happy one and would not harm anyone.

Shortly afterwards, when Mrs. Smith's father died, the pebble showers ceased.

The Ghost Who Hated Women

They say he was a terrible man when he was alive, full of anger and hate. He hasn't improved since he became a ghost.

They call him George, and he inhabits a bedroom on the third floor of the Old Stone House, a little museum in Georgetown, a section of Washington, D.C. The house is reputed to be the oldest building in Washington. It certainly seems to be one of the most haunted. The most violent ghost in the place is called George. He hates women.

The Old Stone House is a national museum, administered by the National Park Service. Rae Koch, the Park Ranger in charge, said that one time George tried to push her over a railing outside his third-floor bedroom. She managed to resist him, and lived to tell the tale.

Often, Rae says, when women try to go into George's room they can't get in. Something seems to be holding them out. Guess who.

George seemed to take a particular dislike to Evelyn, a teenage English girl who worked as a volunteer at the house. Rae says, "When Evelyn would go into that bedroom you could actually see her being pushed out."

There was something about Evelyn that seemed to set George off. And if you were with Evelyn, his anger might spill over on you. One time another member of the staff, Karen Cobb, went up to the third floor with Evelyn. Evelyn began to feel very uncomfortable, as well she might, and left the floor. Perhaps George was frustrated that Evelyn had gotten away.

"When Evelyn left," Karen said later, "the next thing I knew there were hands around my neck, strangling me. I managed to break loose and ran down the stairs. I ran outside. It was like it was pursuing me till I got out into the courtyard. I just collapsed on the bricks. My throat was badly bruised. I've gone up there since, but believe me, not with Evelyn."

Various visitors have seen George. One woman visitor asked, "Who is that man on the third floor with the suspenders?"

A staff volunteer, Peggy Beach, had ancestors who lived in the house before it became a museum. She thinks George is a great-great-grandfather of hers. He often wore suspenders.

"He was an awful man," she says.

6. MALICIOUS GHOSTS

A Dangerous Spirit

When Edd Schultz graduated from divinity school, he became a minister in an Episcopal church in Weymouth, a village near Boston. With his wife Caroline and baby Christopher he moved into an old house on the edge of town.

The house had two apartments on the second floor. There was a stairway between them that led down to the front door of the building. Although summer that year was extremely hot, the stairway was always very cold. It was something the Schultzes didn't think much about—at first.

But mysterious, frightening things soon began to happen. One day Caroline was standing at the top of the stairs, holding the baby. Suddenly she felt hands on the back of her shoulders, pushing her. With the baby, she fell 20 steps down the stairs. As she was falling, she could feel a cold chill around her, but she was aware of a warm glow from the baby in her arms. Neither she nor the baby was hurt.

A week later, during the middle of the night, the baby started screaming from his crib in a nearby room. Edd usually got up during the night to attend to the baby, but Caroline could not awaken him. So she got up and went to see what was wrong.

"As she was leaving our bedroom," Edd recalls, "I woke up. I had what I can only describe as a feeling of tremendous panic. I felt I was being held down by an evil presence. It was as though it was trying to possess me."

After a few moments, Edd managed to free himself and follow his wife down the corridor. She had been having her own experiences. She again felt icy hands on her shoulders. They closed around her neck as though trying to choke her. She broke loose and rushed to the baby's room. She picked him up and managed to calm him.

Edd recalls, "It was such a strong experience that to this day we prefer not to talk about it. It sends shivers up and down our spines."

Edd began to question the landlady about the history of the house. He discovered that the house had originally been a barn where a man had committed suicide by hanging himself from a rafter. His body had hung undiscovered for days, in the space that now was the staircase.

A Very Scary Doll

Can a doll haunt a house?

Take Robert, a large doll that for many years inhabited the Artist House in Key West, an island off the southern tip of Florida. The Artist House is a bed and breakfast establishment, a place to relax, but some patrons have had anything but relaxing times there.

The owner, Ed Cox, tells of a young German woman

who stayed in the front bedroom, and who was terrified. "The more you go up that staircase, the worse the feeling is," she said.

The front bedroom was the place where the doll had been kept for many years.

A plumber working at the Artist House insisted that he heard the doll giggle, and that he found it sitting in different spots when no one was around to move it. Did it move itself?

Owner Cox tells of other disturbances in the house—of pictures that fly off the walls, for example. He once saw the door of a book cabinet spring open for no visible reason. Sometimes doors won't open. Sometimes they open when they shouldn't.

Who is Robert, and what could he be up to?

Robert was the doll of Robert Gene Otto, an artist who lived in the house all his life. When Gene, as he was called, was given the doll he was five years old. It was the custom around 1900 to give a child a doll that looked like him.

Robert the doll is the size of a child. He has human hair, and buttons for eyes. Gene used to dress the doll in his own clothes. He also gave it his first name.

Myrt Reuter, who owned the house after Gene died, cared for Robert as though he were a human being. "It has different kinds of clothes," she said. "It was in a pixie outfit when I got him. Now I have Gene's little sailor suit on him.

"I've been told," she said, "that when Gene did anything mean or hateful he always blamed it on the doll."

Myrt Reuter tells of renting the house to a law student one winter. She says, "He told this story that the doll was voodoo and it locked him up in the attic."

Was that true? Possibly. But it is a fact that many people have reported strange experiences in the house, whether or not Robert was causing them.

Enid Hoffman, who has written books about the Hawaiian mystical tradition, Huna, suspects that what is going on with Robert is what the Hawaiians call Mana.

"Mana," she says, "carries ideas. It can be stored in certain things, wood and silk in particular. It flows in ways that are hard for us to understand. The doll has possibly infected the atmosphere of the house."

Gene had been a bad-tempered person all his life. The doll had been his "mirror image." A lot of his personality had gone into the doll—all the evil thoughts and actions. Possibly Gene's anger is living on after his death, through Robert.

The Demonic Hairdresser

It's distressing enough to get a bad haircut, but when it's a ghost who is giving it to you, it's an even grimmer experience!

That's what happened to a woman in North Carolina, whom we'll call Mary Johnson. Mary woke up one morning to find that her hair had been cut in a random, haphazard, disfiguring way. Parts of her head looked as though they had been shaved. Then it happened again—and again—sometimes even during the day. Mary would go into a sort of trance—she called it a spell—and when she came to, her hair would be cut.

Mary was about 60, and she lived in a small house with her daughter, Jennifer, who was 30. Jennifer began to wonder if she herself were being possessed by a spirit and were giving her mother these haircuts without knowing it. But sometimes Mary would go into her bedroom and lock the door, even nail it shut, and the haircuts would still occur.

The women began to wonder whether the haircuts were coming from Mary's dead husband, Roger, who was Jennifer's father.

Twenty years before, when the family had been living in Ohio, Roger had become involved in black magic. This terrified Mary, and she took the little girl and fled to North Carolina. Roger was bitterly offended. After a time, he followed and moved in with them. A few years later, he died of a heart attack.

Almost immediately after Roger's death, Mary and Jennifer became aware of strange sounds in the house. They heard knockings, footsteps, voices whispering. They saw vague, unrecognizable apparitions and soon the haircuts began.

Finally, in desperation, they called in a woman who was both a psychologist and a psychic. Dr. Jeannie Lagle is a well-trained psychotherapist whose work with clients often has an added dimension. She uses her natural psychic abilities to help her clients. She came to the house, talked with the women, and agreed that it was their husband and father who was causing the trouble.

"What we did was a sort of family therapy," Jeannie relates. "The unusual aspect of it was that one of the people—Roger—had been dead for some years."

The three women began meeting in seances, and, according to Jeannie, the spirit of Roger came and joined in. The seances were not an immediate success. Mary got at least one haircut at this time. But eventually the heart-to-heart talks seemed to calm down Roger's fearsome spirit. In the therapy sessions, Jeannie seemed to convince him that by remaining close to the physical plane and harassing his wife he was doing nobody any good, including himself. It seemed that he took Jeannie's advice and went elsewhere.

Whatever happened to Roger, the haircuts stopped!

7. GHOSTS WHO STAY BEHIND

The Lady and the Time Warp

It was nine o'clock in the morning on a day in 1963 in the White Building on the campus of Wesleyan University, in Lincoln, Nebraska. The corridors were filled with the clatter and chatter of students arriving for their first classes.

Colleen Buterbaugh, secretary to the university dean, had come over from the next building to deliver some papers to the office of a visiting professor from Scotland. She knew that the professor, James McNutt, wasn't in because she had phoned him, but thought she would put the papers on his desk.

When she opened the door to the small office, suddenly everything went quiet. She could no longer hear the noise of the students. In fact, the room itself looked different, somehow strange.

Glancing to the right, she saw a tall young woman with long hair. "It was puffed up," Colleen said, "like they used to wear before World War I. She was wearing a lacy blouse closed at the neck and long sleeves. A long black skirt hung to her ankles, and she was wearing old-time buckle shoes. She was going through a rack of music, apparently looking for something."

The room felt cold and clammy. Colleen looked out the window and felt she was in a different period of time. The tall trees were not tall. They were only a few yards high, as though they had been planted only a few years before. Across from the White Building stood the main library of the university, but it was not there now. There was no building there at all. Colleen felt she was seeing things as they must have looked on the campus 50 years before.

"The woman had her back to me," Colleen said. "She

91

was reaching up into one of the shelves with her right hand and standing perfectly still. She wasn't at all aware of my presence. She never moved. She was not transparent, and yet I knew she wasn't real. While I was looking at her she just faded away—not parts of her body, one at a time, but her whole body at once."

Shaken to the core, Colleen staggered back to the building next door. As her coworkers gathered around to hear her story, an elderly professor said:

"Why, that's a dead ringer for Clara Mills as she looked when she started teaching here." He said that Clara, a professor of music, had begun teaching at the university in 1911, and had died suddenly in her office in 1940.

Colleen was shown old faculty photographs, and she recognized the mysterious, ghostly woman in one of them. It was Clara Mills.

After Colleen's experience, somebody asked James McNutt, the visiting professor from Edinburgh, if he now had any fears about going into his office.

"None at all," said Professor McNutt. "I don't see why Scotland should have a corner on all the ghosts."

When Battles Replay Themselves

Many a person has been frightened out of his or her wits while walking on a deserted moor in England and suddenly spotting a troop of Roman soldiers, in full gear, trudging along. The apparition usually fades quickly, but it's not something a witness is likely to forget.

Such sightings are a longtime tradition in England. After all, it was a couple of thousand years ago that the

Romans were occupying the British Isles, and their apparitions seem to have been there ever since.

These spectres are sometimes called place memories. Somehow a scene has been impressed on the atmosphere and can be viewed at times. It is similar to a picture on a TV screen, for the ghosts never speak to, or even look at, the witnesses. They are not actually the spirits of these long-dead men, they are just images that can occasionally be seen by live people. They are not aware of any earthly surroundings.

One of the most famous of these place memories was observed by hundreds of people in 1642 in Warwickshire. It concerned the Battle of Edgehill, where 14,000 men fought in the English Civil War. Soon after the battle took place, on four weekend nights visitors to the battlefield saw the events "replay" themselves.

A pamphlet was published at the time, which described the scene as follows:

"A great wonder in heaven shewing the late apparitions and prodigious noyse of war and battels, seen on Edge-Hill, neere Keinton, in Northamptonshire 1642."

King Charles I sent representatives to witness these events, and they signed statements swearing that they had actually seen them.

A Hitchhiking Ghost

One day in 1978, a South African army corporal, Dawie Van Jaarsveld, was riding his motorcycle near the town of Uniondale. Suddenly he saw a young woman standing by the side of the road, waving for a ride. He stopped, gave her a spare crash helmet he was carrying, and, smiling, she climbed on the rear seat.

After a few miles, Dawie felt a bumping sensation. He

looked back, and he no longer had a passenger. The spare helmet was strapped to the bike.

Dawie braked his motorcycle to a screeching halt. The area was treeless and there were no houses nearby. There was no cover for a person to hide. And he could see no one lying back on the road. The area was deserted.

Shaken, Dawie stopped at the first place he saw, a small restaurant. There were no customers, but an elderly man stood behind the counter. Dawie stammered out his story of the disappearing young woman.

The old man nodded. He reached behind the counter and pulled out a small photograph, which he held towards the young man. "Did she look like this?" he asked.

Dawie nodded his head. "Yes," he said, "that is her."

"That girl's name is Maria Charlotte Roux," the old man said. "A lot of people have seen her on the road, even given her rides in cars. She sits in the back seat, and then disappears.

"She used to live around here. She was killed in a car crash right down the road. That was ten years ago."

The Hotel Clerk Who Won't Quit

If you take a job at the Kennebunk Inn in Kennebunk, Maine, you've got to be ready to contend with a ghost. And it seems to be a ghost who doesn't know he's dead.

If you're a bartender, you've got to be ready to dodge mugs that fly off the shelves behind the bar. You've got to take it in stride if glasses shatter when nobody is near them.

If you're a waitress or waiter, you might have a full tray of dinners knocked out of your hand. Or you might set up a table and come back a moment later to find a mess—the tablecloth on the floor, silverware scattered, chairs knocked over. And nobody—nobody visible— would have been in the room but yourself

The people at the Kennebunk Inn are used to this. "It's just Cyrus," they say, and they pick up the silverware or rub their heads where the flying beer mug hit them.

When Arthur and Angela LeBlanc bought the inn, they made a number of renovations. As we've seen before, this tends to stir up spirits, who don't like things to change.

One waitress, Pat Butler, happened to be psychic. "That's a ghost," said Pat, "and the name Cyrus keeps coming to me." So they called the ghost Cyrus.

One day a man came in for dinner. He said he had fond memories of the inn, because his uncle had been night clerk there for many years. What was his uncle's name, he was asked. "Cyrus Perkins," he replied.

Cyrus had lived in a room in the basement, so the inn was his home as well as his workplace. His spirit was very active in the cellar. John Bowker, a waiter, says, "You go down to the cellar, and he waits till you get your arms full and then he flicks out the lights."

Many employees of the inn refuse to go down to the cellar.

One summer, the LeBlancs' daughter, Elise, worked at the inn as a waitress. She became friends with two sisters who had come to the inn for a few days because they had heard of the ghost. They brought along a Ouija board, which is a device that supposedly spells out messages from spirits. But take warning, it can be dangerous to use. Sometimes it can bring in unpleasant spirits.

Elise says: "We took it down to the basement. The rule was no hands on the thing. We just held our hands over the board, about a half-inch above the planchette, which is the thing that moves around and spells out words. And it really moved! It was freaky! It scared me! I've never gone near a Ouija board except for that one time.

"We asked the ghost how old he was when he died. The planchette wouldn't move. I got an idea. I said, maybe he doesn't know he's dead. So we asked him if he was dead, and the planchette went to NO!"

A Sight Not on
the Program

During the 1880s, a man and his wife were attending a performance at the Lyceum Theater, a well-known theater in London at the time. They were sitting in a box, which looked down at the seats on the floor. During the first intermission, the man happened to glance down, and he saw a ghastly sight.

A woman was sitting in a floor seat, wearing a flowing

silk gown. The man looked again and then stared intently. For in her lap there appeared to be the disembodied head of a man! It seemed to belong to a person who might have lived a couple of centuries before. It had long hair, a moustache, and a pointed beard. The head looked deathly pale, as though it had just been chopped off!

The shaken witness pointed out the sight to his wife. Yes, she could see it too. The lights were just going down for the second act of the play. Even though the couple were fearful, they were even more curious. They left their box and went down to the floor to see if they could get closer to the woman. They were able to get close enough to see that the grisly object now seemed to be covered by a silk wrap in the woman's lap.

They went back to their box. At the end of the play they tried to speak to the woman, but they missed her in the exiting crowd. However, a sight such as this, especially the features of the head, remained fixed in their memories.

The man was a dealer in paintings. Some years later, he had occasion to travel to Yorkshire to evaluate some pictures. While in a stockroom, he unwrapped one particular painting, and gasped! For it was a portrait of the man whose head he had seen in the lady's lap all those years before.

Making inquiries, he found that the portrait was of a

member of the family of the Earl of Essex. The Essex family had once owned the ground on which the Lyceum Theater had later been built. This particular man had been executed during the regime of Oliver Cromwell, a time when many aristocrats had met a similar fate. His head had been chopped off.

A part of the man—in both the physical and ghostly sense—had remained in this familiar site.

It is most doubtful that the woman in the theater had any awareness of the gruesome object she was holding in her lap!

8. BETRAYAL AND MURDER

The Ghost Who Came Back for Justice

Sometimes a ghost will stay in our physical world to see that justice is done, that its good name is cleared. Richard Tarwell was such a ghost.

Tarwell, a 14-year-old boy, worked in the kitchen of a large country house in England, in the year 1730. The owner, George Harris, also had a house in London. One day Harris received a message from Richard Morris, the butler of his country home. Morris said that the house had been broken into the night before and a large amount of valuable silverware had been stolen.

Harris returned, and got the whole story. Morris said he had been awakened in the night by a noise. He hurried to the butler's pantry, where the silverware was kept, and was confronted by two rough-looking thieves. With them, the butler said, was the young boy Tarwell, who it appeared had let them in.

Butler Morris said that the men had overpowered him and tied him up. Then they and the boy removed all the silver and left for parts unknown. Morris had been found by his fellow servants the next morning, none the worse for wear.

Some months later, George Harris awoke to see a young boy standing by his bed. He realized it was Tarwell. He presumed the boy had been hiding in the house since the robbery.

The boy said nothing, just beckoned. As the lad moved, making no sound at all, Harris realized he was seeing a ghost. He followed the boy out of the house to a large oak tree. The ghost pointed to the ground, and then disappeared.

The next morning, Harris had workmen dig where the ghost had pointed. They found the body of Richard Tarwell.

Police were called, and they interrogated the butler, who confessed. He was part of the robbery plot, having let the thieves in himself. While they were taking the silver, the boy Tarwell had heard a noise and investigated. One of the robbers struck the boy and killed him. To cover the crime, they buried Tarwell and tied up their accomplice, the butler, to hide his participation in the robbery.

Even though he was now a ghost, Tarwell was not going to let the butler get away with his death and the ruin of his reputation.

He was successful. The butler was hanged for the crime.

The Silent Witness

Many small children can see ghosts that the adults around them cannot see. Usually, they do not speak of these visions, for they have learned that grown-ups will rebuke them, will tell them they are making things up.

Irma was five years old in the summer of 1936. She and

her family were staying at a resort hotel in the Canadian Rockies. One day two beautiful young people checked in. The man was tall and solidly built. The woman was short and slim. They seemed very much in love. The gossip went that they were on their honeymoon.

Irma was told they were champion swimmers, and had come here to put the final touches on their training for the Olympic games, which were to be held a few weeks later in Berlin. They would go off every day and swim in the surrounding lakes and rivers.

One morning at breakfast they mentioned that they were going to swim to a small island not far away. A waiter, who lived year-round in the area, overheard them and warned them to be careful. There was a very strong whirlpool near that island, with a powerful under-tow. Over the years, several people had been drowned there, he said.

The young man merely smiled, and glanced about the table as if saying, "These local people always have their stories."

A few minutes later, they left the hotel in their swim-suits, laughing, as though they didn't have a care in the world.

An hour later, the man came stumbling back alone. He seemed exhausted, and in such a dire emotional state that he was weeping and throwing up. He gasped out a tale that his wife had been caught in the whirlpool and that he had been unable to find her.

The entire hotel was thrown into a frenzy of anguish. A search party was organized, but the young woman's body was never found.

Little Irma had a question all her own. For when the man returned, she could see his young wife standing behind him. She was wearing a wet bathing suit and was doubled over as if in pain. She was crying, "How could you? How could you?"

Irma tagged along with the search party, and all the time she could see the drowned woman behind her husband, tears running down her cheeks. Even when the group returned to the hotel, the little girl could see the young woman a few feet from her husband.

This continued all summer for Irma. She could stand on a high place near the hotel and look across the water at the island. She could see the young woman on its shore, bent over as though in pain, as though she had been hit in the stomach. And even at that distance, Irma could hear her cry:

"Why did he do it? I loved him!"

The Party Stopper

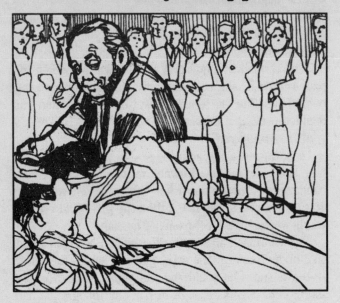

The young couple were throwing a house-warming party. They had bought the house, in Vancouver, Canada, only a few months before. The time was the 1930s.

They had bought the house from a middle-aged man who seemed in great haste to get away from the place. In any case, he was selling the house at a price well below its market value. The young couple were mystified as to why he would let this handsome house go at such a low price, but they congratulated themselves at their good fortune, and closed the deal.

As they made friends with the neighbors, they discovered that the man's wife had died in the house a short time before.

"Ah," said the young woman, "he probably was so devastated by her death that he had to get away from these familiar surroundings, with all their memories."

The neighbor shook her head. "I would doubt that," she said. "Their marriage was collapsing. In fact, towards the end they seemed to hate each other."

The young couple moved in happily, but soon they felt an uneasiness in the place that they could not explain. They tried to ignore it, and went about doing renovations, tearing down walls, buying new furniture, putting their own stamp on the place. When they had completed their changes, they sent out invitations for a party, feeling that such an occasion would make the place more their own.

The party was fully under way, with laughter, banter, food and drink. A small band was tuning up to play for dancing.

All at once, an icy chill pervaded the living room. A frightened gasp went up from the group. A woman guest screamed, then another. For at one end of the room a ghastly scene had appeared. A silent scene, as though from a silent theatre.

On a massive bed lay a woman. She seemed struggling in the throes of death. Her eyes blazed with fear and anger. She appeared to be aghast, as though she had just discovered a terrible truth.

On a chair next to the bed sat a man. He was meeting the woman's glare with a small, tight smile, as though he were congratulating himself, and taunting her.

The young host and hostess gripped each other. For this spectre looked exactly like the man who had sold them the house. Many of the people at the party were neighbors, and they recognized the dying woman as the man's wife.

The vision was seen by the entire company for a brief—although seemingly endless—moment. Then it faded as silently as it had appeared.

The party ended instantly. The band was dismissed, the dancing cancelled. One of the neighbors, saying her goodbyes to the host and hostess, commented that this room had been the older couple's bedroom during the time they had lived in the house. The young couple nodded awkwardly.

Within a week, they had sold the house, including their new furniture, and had moved out.

The Waltz of Death

When the West was still wild, one of the few spots of civilization in New Mexico was Fort Union. This military post was manned by rugged soldiers and many young officers. They were very lonely, for there were few women in these parts.

One day a beautiful young woman, a niece of the commandant, came for an extended visit. Every man on the post fell in love with Miranda. This did not make her unhappy. There was little there to interest her except for men, and flirting was her favorite pastime.

One day a very young lieutenant, just out of West Point, was posted to the fort. He immediately fell madly in love with Miranda. For her, he was a new toy.

Fort Union was established to guard pioneers against the Apache Indians, who themselves were fighting to protect their homes and land. One day the young lieutenant was ordered to lead a small party against the Apaches. That night the young man pledged his undying love to Miranda. She answered in kind, hiding a yawn. As though playing a stage role, she murmured, "I will never marry another man."

"That is well," the young man said, "for whatever happens, I will come back and make my claim."

The scouting party was ambushed by the Apaches. Very few soldiers escaped back to the fort, and the lieutenant was not among them. Miranda showed little sign of sorrow. In fact, secretly she was relieved. Within weeks, she announced that she was leaving to marry a rich man back East.

The people of Fort Union held a going-away party. Everyone came in their best clothes. Miranda danced with one man after another.

Suddenly there was a bang! A door had flown open. A cold wind swept the room. A soldier's wife screamed and dropped to the floor in a faint. For a figure stood at the door. An unearthly cry came from its lips as it staggered forward into the light. It was the young lieutenant. His body was swollen, his uniform stained with blood. His scalp was gone. His eyes burned with a terrible light.

The figure lurched towards Miranda and took the terrified, rigid young woman in its arms. Faster and faster they danced! Miranda grew paler and paler. She slipped to the floor. The ghastly figure stood over her. The lights went out.

When the candles were lit again, the figure was gone. Miranda lay dead.

A few days later, a search party returned to the fort. They brought with them, over the back of a horse, the body of the young lieutenant.

9. MURDER
WILL OUT

The Boy with the
Brass Buttons

The old-fashioned house in Stuyvesant Square caught the eye of a young couple who had just arrived in Philadelphia that winter day in 1889. They bought it and moved in with their little six-year-old daughter.

There was a lot of refurbishing to be done, so it was nice to have an attic in which the little girl could play while the rest of the house was being worked on. The previous owners, the Cowderys, had turned the attic into a playroom. It even had a fireplace, though it was now boarded up.

After a couple of weeks, the downstairs rooms were finished. The mother, realizing she hadn't seen much of her daughter in the past fortnight, planned to spend more time with her. But the little girl wasn't interested. She kept stealing away to the attic.

"What's so interesting up there in that stuffy room?" the exasperated mother asked at last.

"It's the little boy with the shiny buttons," the child replied. "He's so much fun to play with."

"What little boy?" her mother demanded, wondering if a servant's child had somehow stowed away in the room. She went to investigate. But the room was empty.

Certain that her daughter was just being stubborn, the mother appealed to her husband to discipline the child. At her father's stern voice, the little girl became hysterical. She kept repeating that there was a little boy and that he wore a blue jacket with lots of shiny buttons on it.

As her father listened, he became more and more

curious. Formerly a seaman, he recognized her description of the buttons. They were probably brass and part of a child's sailor suit. He made some inquiries about the Cowderys, the family who had lived in the house before him. He learned that they had come from England with their children, two boys and a girl. The youngest child, a boy, was retarded. The neighbors described him as an idiot child.

According to the boy's parents, they went on, the young boy had always loved the nearby river. One day he had sneaked away on his own to play on its banks. He had fallen into the water and drowned. His body was never recovered, but his cap had been found floating on the river. Shortly after the child's disappearance, the Cowderys put the house up for sale and, leaving Philadelphia, dropped out of sight.

The former seaman's suspicions were now thoroughly aroused. He accompanied his little daughter to the attic and asked her to show him where the boy came from. She pointed to the boarded-up fireplace. Her father called in workers to open it and then to remove the mortar that cemented up a cavity in the wall beside the chimney.

As the mortar was chipped away, the corpse of a small boy was revealed. He was clothed in a little blue sailor jacket with four rows of brass buttons down the front. Examination showed that the back of the child's skull had been crushed.

No accidental drowning! Cold-blooded murder!

The Cursed Weed Patch

In 1821, John Newton of Newtown, Montgomeryshire, Wales, was brought to trial for murder. He vehemently proclaimed his innocence. But his protestations were ignored. He was convicted on purely circumstantial evidence and the testimony of two Welshmen who, Newton claimed, would profit from his death.

It was all to no avail. He was convicted and the judge sentenced him to death by hanging. Staring at the judge, his eyes burning, Newton shouted, "I am innocent! And to prove my innocence I will allow no grass to grow on my grave forever!"

John Newton was hanged in a public ceremony that, strangely enough, took place in a sudden fierce thunderstorm that filled the onlookers with misgivings. After the hanging, his corpse was buried in the country church-yard. The grave was unmarked by any headstone. All the same, it was easy to pick out. Among all the green graves in the cemetery, it alone was covered with sprawling weeds that followed the oblong pattern of the coffin lying below.

The unseemly grave appeared to be proclaiming the innocence of the dead man. To blot out a growing sense of guilt in the little town, officials realized that if grass was going to grow on the grave, they'd have to make it happen themselves. Rich soil was brought in and spread over the grave. Grass seeds were planted. The soil was then watered and tended carefully. But none of the seeds sprouted. The patch of unsightly weeds remained.

By 1852 the Reverend Robert Mostyn Price took up the cause of the hanged man.

"Thirty years have passed," he wrote, "and we cannot grow any grass on this grave. I and others believe that this is proof that the poor man was innocent."

But it's difficult for human beings to accept the fact that justice has miscarried and caused the death of an innocent man. Once again an effort was made to grow grass on Newton's grave. Fresh rich soil was spread. The finest and hardiest grass seeds known were sown there, and the little plot was again carefully watered and tended.

A few grass shoots sprang up, but they were quickly

smothered by a fresh crop of straggly weeds. The ugly little patch continued to stand out starkly in the lush green expanse of the graveyard.

Even over a century later, in 1941, a visitor to the cemetery was able to pick out the spot at once. The coffin-sized patch of weeds was still there among the green, neatly manicured graves of its sleeping companions, giving mute testimony to justice gone awry and a Welshman's curse!

Ghost with the Bloodstained Hands

I'll call them Jan and Mark Jackson, because they don't want any publicity about their weird experience. It was 1965 when it took place. The couple was living in an apartment on the third floor of an old Colonial-style house on Decatur Street in the French Quarter of New Orleans. Jan and Mark loved their apartment, with its charming, old-fashioned air. They didn't even mind most of the strange things that kept happening.

For instance, the clock on the living room mantel kept stopping every night at 3 A.M. and had to be reset every morning. And sometimes the Jacksons glimpsed a couple of shadowy figures that vanished as quickly as they appeared.

But there was one ghost that made them shiver. It was the ghost of a young woman in a filmy white gown that kept drifting through the rooms, her pleading eyes wide with shock and horror, her bloodstained hands clasped against her breast. This ghost upset the Jacksons so much that they began to ask questions about the old house. The answers led them to a story about something that had happened in the apartment back in 1910. At that time a young married woman was renting the Jacksons' apartment, where she was secretly meeting her lover. One day both she and her lover disappeared. It was suspected that the woman's jealous husband had found out about the affair and murdered them. But since the bodies were never found, there could also be another simpler explanation—one that the husband suggested—that the two had simply run away together.

So, after the first flurry of headlines, the newspapers had dropped the subject and the story was forgotten.

Because of the ghost with the bloodstained hands, the Jacksons were convinced it was a case of murder and that the bodies had been hidden somewhere nearby. But where? Mark got his answer the day he went up to the attic to get something he had stored away.

In a corner, he noticed several rotted floorboards. Planning to replace them, he pulled them out and found himself looking down at two skeletons in the space below. Lying side by side, they were grinning up at him with gaping jaws. On the rib cage of one lay the blood-encrusted knife that must have killed them.

The Jacksons talked it over and decided that since both murderer and murdered were long dead, there would be no purpose in announcing their find. That night, they secretly buried the skeletons in a single grave. From that time on, the ghost with the bloodstained hands walked no more. And the clock on the mantel—that had obviously been marking the hour of the murder—continued ticking the night through.

The Most Honored Ghost

The most famous phantom in all Australia is the ghost of Frederick George James Fisher of Campbelltown, New South Wales, who was murdered in 1826. Fisher was a convict sent to Australia for a minor offense. He made good in his new country as the first man to manufacture paper in New South Wales. And he accumulated enough capital to purchase a 30-acre farm watered by a stream that flowed through his property.

The land next to Fisher's was rented by George Worrall, another convict settler. The two men became close friends. For a time Fisher even lived at Worrall's home.

Then, on June 17, 1826, Fisher suddenly disappeared. Worrall explained that his friend had run away to England to escape a charge of forgery that was being brought against him. Meanwhile, Worrall claimed that, in his absence, Fisher had made him overseer of his estate.

As time went on, Worrall began taking more and more liberties with Fisher's possessions. People began whispering about murder, especially when Worrall tried selling a horse that had belonged to Fisher. The whispers grew louder when he tried to sell some timber he had taken from a grove of trees on Fisher's property. Finally, Worrall offered to pay $80 for the title deed to Fisher's land, which was being held against a debt Fisher owed a man named Daniel Cooper.

But suspicions are only suspicions and there was still no real proof that Fisher had not fled to England as Worrall claimed.

Then one day a special constable named Farley was walking along the fence that separated Fisher's farm from Worrall's. He was startled to see a man either climbing or leaning against the fence in the southeastern corner of the Fisher property. The man's face was turned towards the creek, but Farley recognized the figure as Fisher. As Farley watched, Fisher raised his arm, pointing his forefinger in the direction of the creek.

Astonished at the man's sudden return, Farley called out Fisher's name. At this, the figure vanished. Farley hurried to the section of the fence where he had seen the ghost. Examining the rails, he saw massive blood stains.

With this new information, a concentrated search was made for Fisher's corpse. On October 20, 1826, two state troopers uncovered it in a swampy section of the creek bank, exactly where the ghost had pointed. Worrall was taken into custody, tried, convicted and hanged in February, 1827.

As for Farley, any suspicion that he might have made up the story to urge on the investigation was dispelled as he lay dying in 1841. When asked by reporters if he had concocted the story, he replied, "I'm a dying man. I'll speak only the truth. I saw that ghost as plainly as I see you now."

Fisher's body was buried in the graveyard of St. Peter's Church in Campbelltown. The grave was unmarked, and today its exact location is unknown. But Fisher's ghost is not forgotten. A festival to celebrate its appearance was first held in Campbelltown in 1856. Since then, the week-long festival in honor of the ghost has been held every year or two. A Fisher's Ghost Ball and other entertainments do honor to the age-old phantom. He is probably the only ghost in the world who is honored with a festival.

10. MYSTIFYING!

Burned Up

Dr. E. J. Sullivan always thought the statement "It burned me up" was only a metaphor. In his case it turned out to be much more.

It was April 24, 1970. Dr. Sullivan, a retired U.S. Naval Commander, had just lost his beloved wife of many years and had spent the day making the final funeral arrangements. Overcome with grief and a kind of hopeless fury at his loss, he flung himself on the bed in his hotel room and gave himself up to a despair so deep that he blanked out.

He lay there, lost in a trancelike state, until he was roused by the ringing of his telephone. He tried to get up to answer it, but found he couldn't move. He could not even open his hands, which were clenched into fists. He looked at them in shock. They were covered with huge blisters that spread up his arms. His feet and legs were also covered with blisters. Instead of feeling pain, his hands, arms, feet and legs had lost all sensation of any kind.

Unable to move, he could only cry out for help. At last, a hotel worker heard him and broke into the room. Sullivan asked to have his personal physician, Dr. George M. Lawton, called in. Dr. Lawton diagnosed the blisters as having been caused by electrical burns, though he couldn't understand how that could have happened. Sullivan had not been near any kind of electrical outlet, and the covers of the bed on which he lay had not even been scorched. The burns were so serious, however, that Dr. Lawton ordered his patient to a hospital.

As they waited for the ambulance to arrive, Sullivan

noticed the time on his watch. It was six o'clock the evening of April 25. Twenty-four hours had gone by since he had flung himself on the bed in his hotel room.

The burns on Dr. Sullivan's hands turned out to be so deep that they destroyed his ability to grip things. This damage appeared to be permanent, despite many hours of physical therapy. Dr. Sullivan was at a loss to explain the mystery. At last, he could account for it only by one extraordinary answer. His fury and despair at losing his wife had literally burned him up with an emotion so fiery, it had emblazoned the deep electrical burns on his body.

The Runaway Locomotive

In January of 1892 engineer J. M. Pinkney visited his friend, a seasoned engineer on the old Northern Pacific Eastbound Overland train. Pinkney's friend covered a stretch of track that crosses the Cascade Mountains of the northwest United States.

As the friends sat together in the engineer's cab of the locomotive, they regaled each other with harrowing accounts of accidents that had occurred on their lines. Pinkney enjoyed most of the stories, but he couldn't take them seriously when they featured the paranormal. As hardheaded a man as you could find, he certainly didn't believe in ghosts.

As the train neared Eagle Gorge, the most dangerous spot on the 2,500-mile run, the engineer embarked on the story of old Tom Cypher. Cypher, he said, was an engineer who had died in an accident here two years before.

Suddenly, the engineer grasped the throttle and threw it over, reversing the engine. Then he applied the air brakes, bringing the train to a standstill. The spot where he had stopped was just a few feet short of the place where Cypher had met his death.

Pinkney couldn't understand why the engineer had stopped the train. There had been no hint of any danger. The night was clear and the track was empty. The engineer explained vaguely that some of the machinery had shaken loose and had to be tightened. In a few minutes, he said, they would be on their way.

As they started forward once more, Pinkney pointed

out that there had been nothing wrong with the machinery, so why the stop?

"Look there!" his friend told him. "Don't you see it?"

Staring out of the cab window, Pinkney saw the headlights of a locomotive just 300 yards ahead. Shocked, he automatically reached for the lever to stop the train. His friend pushed his hand away, laughing.

"It's only old Tom Cypher's engine, No. 33," he said. 'We won't collide. Because that man at the throttle is Cypher himself and, dead though he may be, he can go faster backwards than any man alive can go forwards. I've seen it 20 times before. Every engineer on this road looks for it."

Pinkney felt the hairs on his neck stand up as he watched the engine ahead of them, its headlights throwing out rays of red, green and white light. It had begun running silently backwards, remaining only a short distance ahead of them. Pinkney glimpsed a shadowy figure at the throttle. Then the locomotive rounded a curve and disappeared from view.

The train on which Pinkney was riding now began passing several small stations. At each one, the station master, fearful of an impending collision, warned the engineer to watch out for a runaway engine, No. 33, that was travelling backwards just a short distance ahead of them.

The engineer only laughed. "It's just old Cypher playing a prank," he said.

Pinkney still couldn't believe that a ghost had been at the throttle of that locomotive. Worried, he sent a telegram to the next station, which was in the town of Sprague, asking if No. 33 with a daredevil engineer aboard had been stopped.

The strange reply came back. "Rogue locomotive No. 33 has just arrived, her coal exhausted, her boxes burned out. No engineer at the throttle."

The Phantom Biplane

On May 27, 1963, Sir Peter Masefield, well known in aviation lore, was flying a DeHavilland Chipmunk from Dalcross to Shoreham, England. Masefield was going by way of the abandoned RAF airfield at Montrose. As he approached the airfield, he suddenly saw before him an ancient biplane, a plane with two pairs of supporting wings placed one above the other. It was the type of plane the RAF used for training before World War I.

The plane was close enough so that Masefield could see the aviator, who was dressed in a leather helmet, goggles and the silken scarf that was part of every old-time aviator's wardrobe. As Masefield stared, the biplane's upper right wing broke loose from its struts. The craft spun crazily in midair and then spiralled to the ground and crashed.

In horror, Masefield landed at a nearby golf course among a group of startled players. He shouted to them for help. Though the golfers had heard and seen nothing of a crash, they followed Sir Peter to the abandoned airfield. It was empty.

The experience was so disturbing to Masefield that he made inquiries at the Accidents Investigation Committee headquarters of the RAF. He found two entries dated June 2 and June 10, 1913. They described an accident that had taken place on the 27th of May, 1913. A training plane flown by Lieutenant Desmond Arthur had lost its upper right wing and crashed at Montrose field on that date.

Young Lieutenant Arthur was Irish, from County Clare. When he died, he was given a burial with full military honors. But in 1916 an official report attributed the loss of his plane to negligence and his memory was blackened.

From that time on, the ghost of Lieutenant Arthur was seen at No. 2 Mess Hall, where he had lived. It was always dressed in the full uniform of an aviator. It appeared so often that it became known as the "Irish Apparition."

Soon the ghost began to show up in other parts of the base. When guards challenged the ghost, it would disappear before their eyes, sending them fleeing in terror.

The story of the ghost spread through the RAF and beyond. It began appearing in newspapers across England, where it came to the attention of an editor for a British flying magazine. He concluded that the dead aviator wanted his name cleared and insisted that the RAF make a further investigation into the cause of the crash. This time the RAF found that the blame lay not on the aviator but on the poor maintenance of the aircraft. The honor of the dead aviator restored, the Irish Apparition made its last appearance on earth in January of 1917.

But the daredevil young pilot must have still been haunting the airwaves above Montrose, when on May

27, 1963—the fiftieth anniversary of his death—he repeated his spectacular crash for the benefit of Sir Peter Masefield, one of Great Britain's most renowned aviators.

Jinxed Ship

One day in 1869 a workman was inspecting a fishing schooner, the *Charles Haskell*, for possible damage. He slipped on the steps of the companionway leading to the hold, fell and broke his neck, dying instantly. A single mishap like this usually is chalked up to carelessness or coincidence. But this happened in Newfoundland, Canada, where fishermen who face the dangers of northern waters are likely to take every accident aboard ship as a sign that it is jinxed or cursed.

Certainly, the captain and crew of the *Haskell* believed this. They deserted the ship immediately.

The owner, unable to find anyone willing to sign on, sold the schooner to a Captain Curtis of Gloucester, Massachusetts. The captain was a no-nonsense man who didn't believe in curses. He had some difficulty finding men to work for him at first, but the pay he offered was good and soon he had a crew. The *Charles Haskell* was back fishing again on the Grand Banks, a series of shoals off Newfoundland.

Everything went well until 1870, when a hurricane struck the Grand Banks. The hundred or so fishing ships gathered there were tossed about like matchsticks. One huge comber lifted the *Charles Haskell* and hurled it like a battering ram against the *Andrew Johnson*, which was smashed to pieces, killing everyone aboard. Though badly crippled, the *Haskell* managed to limp back to port.

Most fishermen would have considered that part of the *Haskell's* curse. But since it was the *Andrew Johnson* that went down, the crew felt it didn't apply to them.

Once the ship was repaired, it was back on the Grand Banks again.

For six days the crew of the *Charles Haskell* fished without incident. But on midnight of the seventh day, the watchmen standing guard spied movement in the waters around the ship. As they watched, 26 figures wearing rain slickers began rising out of the sea. One by one, they boarded the schooner. Staring straight ahead through eyeless sockets, they took up stations along the ship's railing. There they went through the motions of fishing.

Frozen with terror, the guards were unable to move until the phantoms put away their imaginary nets and fishing rods and returned back to the sea. Then they rushed to the captain's cabin, gabbling out an account of what they had seen.

Captain Curtis couldn't understand a word they were saying. But he saw stark fear in their eyes and ordered the ship back to port at once. It was well on its way by dawn. In the bright light of day the night's terrors seemed foolish. The captain was on the verge of returning to the Grand Banks when one of the crew shouted, "Look!"

Gaping, captain and crew watched as the 26 figures in rain slickers again rose from the sea and boarded the schooner. Once more they took up fishing positions along the rail. Finding his voice at last, the captain ordered full sail for port. But fast as the ship went, it could not shake the phantom fishermen. They stayed aboard until the port finally came into view. Then they climbed over the side of the ship. But this time, instead of sinking into the sea, they started walking across the sparkling waters towards the port, where they disappeared.

Who were they? Demons from the deep? The drowned men of the *Andrew Johnson*? No one took the time to ask. As soon as they docked, captain and crew fled, never to return.

No others came to take their place. The *Charles Haskell* was left to rot away in its berth. It never sailed again.

11. WHERE EVIL LURKS

The Power at Nagoon Park

In the daytime Nagoon Park seems a pleasant enough place, lying about four miles away from the town of Manistee on the western side of Lake Michigan. It's woodsy with meadowlands, the home of birds and squirrels, bright and busy. But at dusk a different atmosphere settles over the silent haunted acres. Then it becomes dark and foreboding. There are accounts of lights flickering, jumbles of voices and the screams of a woman and children, riding on sudden gusts of wind that seem to rise from nowhere.

Brian Williams, a newcomer to town, had heard all kinds of stories about the park. Some said it was once the sacred haunt of ancient Indian shamans, who practiced their secret rituals in it. Others spoke of a witches' cult performing strange ceremonies there after dark. And then there was the horrible account of a farmer who once lived there with his wife and a brood of children. One night, in a mad rage, the farmer murdered the whole family, swinging right and left with a bloody axe.

Whatever the reason, all agreed on the dark nature of the park. So bad was its reputation that the city ordered it closed at dusk, the only park in the whole area that was shut down after sunset.

When Brian first heard all these stories, he was amused by them. Well educated and with a college degree, he was not given to what he considered superstition. One day he decided to put a period to all the town lore with a little commonsense action. He'd drive out to Nagoon Park at dusk and prove there was nothing in the tales. Though the park was closed, he'd get as close to it as possible and spend the night.

It wasn't hard to find other recruits—his girlfriend and another skeptical young couple. They decided to make a lark of it. At dusk they piled into Brian's car and drove down the country road in high spirits, stopping as close to the park entrance as they could.

Outside the car all was silent and motionless. The dark shapes of trees in the park hovered high against the sky like a wall, vague, menacing. The air had an uncanny stillness. The heavy silence seemed to flow out of the park like a thick tide. The voices of the young people sounded loud in the night. There was a shrill, almost hysterical cackle to their laughter.

Then, in the stillness, something outrageous happened. The rear of the car started to rise. The couples fell silent, staring at one another. Was it their imagination? Surely it couldn't really be happening.

Higher and higher rose the back of the car. Brian found himself sliding against the steering wheel, staring down at the hood, which was slanting noticeably downwards. And still the rear of the car kept rising until it was some four or five feet above the ground and almost perpendicular to the road. It would have taken a crane to lift the car, yet the country road was silent and deserted.

Then, all at once, the car was dropped. It fell with a

crash. The girl on the back seat was flung against the top of the car. She had been too shocked to utter a sound before, but now she began howling with pain and terror. Brian was shaking as he turned the key in the ignition. The car started! He raced it down the dirt road back to Manistee.

Brian has never returned to Nagoon Park. And he no longer laughs at the tales told about it. He has his own story now.

The Portrait

A few years after World War I, a prominent Boston artist was a house guest in the home of a Mr. Izzard. He was given the best room in the old family mansion that stood on the outskirts of Boston. It was a large bedroom on the top floor with side windows that looked out on landscaped gardens.

The first night he was awakened suddenly by a brilliant glow that hurt his eyes and made his flesh crawl. In that light he saw a woman in an elegant gown standing at the side of the room. Fascinated, he watched as she hurled something out of the window. He couldn't see what it was.

Then the woman turned around and looked at him. She would have been beautiful if her face had not been set in such hard, cruel lines. Dark, malignant eyes flashed their hatred. Her lips were pursed in a smirk of triumph. As that gloating face stared at him, the light and figure slowly faded and disappeared.

The next two nights the horrible vision repeated itself. After the third appearance, the artist felt compelled to sketch the face of the woman he had seen. Later he showed the drawing to his city friends. Everyone was disturbed by the evil in it.

Several months later, Mr. Izzard again invited the artist to his home. This time he led his friend through a gallery of portraits of his ancestors.

The artist stopped suddenly before one of the paintings. It was the portrait of a beautiful and demure young woman.

"I've met her somewhere I'm sure," he exclaimed. "I'd know that face anywhere—only—"

Mr. Izzard laughed. "You couldn't have known her," he said. "She's been dead for a hundred years. She was my great-grandfather's second wife and she certainly was no credit to the family."

He went on to explain that his great-grandfather's

first wife had died, leaving behind her little son. His second wife, having given birth to her own son, was filled with jealousy, sure the family property would go to the older boy. One day his crumpled body was found below the window of the bedroom where the artist had seen the vision. The child had died instantly of a broken neck.

"She was suspected of having murdered him," Mr. Izzard explained. "But nothing could ever be proved."

"It can now," the artist exclaimed. Describing what he had seen, he went to get the drawing he had made.

To his horror, Mr. Izzard saw that the features of the woman in the sketch were the exact features of the woman in the portrait.

Haunted Ferreby House

Sometimes greed reaches even beyond the grave. Perhaps this is what happened in the case of the mansion known as Hopsfield. It got its name because it stood in the middle of a field of hops outside the town of Waterlooville in Hampshire, England.

A huge, rambling Gothic-style house, it was built by a Ferreby in the early 1800s. Proud of his mansion, which boasted a long flight of stone steps to the front door, Mr. Ferreby was determined to have it stay in his family forever: It must never change hands. It would always be home to the Ferrebys. That was his dying wish.

The Ferreby offspring lived in the house and raised their children in it. But when the grandchildren were grown, and their parents had died, they wanted nothing to do with the old place. The rooms had always seemed dank and cold and the atmosphere was heavy and oppressive.

After moving out, the Ferrebys rented the house to a group of Spiritualists, who weren't there long before they began complaining that the ghost of old Mr. Ferreby kept appearing, shaking with anger and threatening them. They were so terrified that they asked for and received permission to sublet the house.

The new occupants were a widow and her daughter, then in her twenties. They stayed only a short while. The mother was found dead in her bed at one o'clock in the morning. Soon afterwards, the daughter moved out of the grim old house, which by this time had begun to get a sorry reputation.

No one else wanted to rent the house. But the Ferreby heirs were able to sell it. It was bought almost immediately by a newly retired sea captain and his wife. One of the captain's treasures was a collection of Indian daggers he had gathered on his travels. He now kept them in a display case in the hall of the Ferreby house.

One morning the sea captain was found lying dead in the front hall, one of his Indian daggers buried in his back. His widow moved out immediately, leaving behind a mystery that the police couldn't solve. Only the local people claimed to know what had happened: Old Ferreby's ghost, long in his uneasy grave, was the killer.

By this time no local person would think of going near the old house. But in the 1920s it caught the eye of the Dalton family, who were determined to buy it even against the advice of advisors and friends. The old Gothic-style building appealed to Mr. Dalton. The dark gloominess of its interior, he said, was the result of neglect. The rooms could be renovated and the atmosphere improved. He poured money into the house, transforming it into a beautiful and luxurious home, but he was never able to get rid of the strange chill that seemed to pervade it.

Overnight guests of the Daltons remember uneasy nights—strange noises, doors that were opened by invisible hands, children who woke in the middle of the night to find themselves crammed under their beds. And everyone still complained of the cold, oppressive atmosphere that no amount of renovations could change.

But there was no discussing these things with the Daltons. They had ready explanations: Children do strange things in their sleep; old houses settle at night, making noises of all kinds; doors come open under the pressure of drafts. The dank, chill atmosphere was just the psychological effect of all those scary stories.

Then one summer Dalton's son, a brilliant young man attending Oxford—with everything apparently going for him—went into the basement of the old house with a gun and blew out his brains. A few weeks later his grieving mother died. Not long after that Mr. Dalton himself suddenly dropped dead in his dressing room. Only one child remained, a daughter. She moved out at once. The magnificently renovated house was boarded up and left empty. No one went near it now. Cold and grim, it stood alone in the field of hops. Did old Mr. Ferreby have his wish at last?

Madness in the Museum

The Gothic-style building that houses the Fremantle Museum in Western Australia was built in 1863 by convicts as an asylum for the mentally ill. During its heyday it was crowded with these sufferers, among them some who were criminally insane.

In 1963, when the vacated buildings were turned into a museum and art center, the rooms were enlarged and modernized and used to display historical relics.

Despite the renovations, the ghosts of those who once lived and died here still seem to haunt the halls. Papers, mops and dusters are sometimes snatched from the hands of employees and tossed around the floor. Knocking is heard in the walls. Footsteps echo up and down the halls.

But the most terrifying things happen in the Discovery Gallery on the second floor. Its story is a dark one. It once contained a block of eight small cells in which violent patients were housed. One of the cells has been preserved to show how badly the criminally insane were treated in the past. The small, cramped cell is equipped with a heavy wooden door that was bolted from the outside.

One day in the late 1970s, a school teacher was taking a group of students through the museum. As she entered the Discovery Gallery, she suddenly began to shove, push and struggle as though she were being attacked by an unseen assailant. All the while she was unable to speak or to hear the questions of her terrified students. At last a museum official was able to lead the teacher out of the room.

The story of the teacher's experience came to the ears of a brash young man who had just been hired by the museum and was visiting it for the first time. We'll call him Alan. He decided he would prove that there were no such things as ghosts by going to the Discovery Gallery and even entering the model cell. But he had no sooner entered the Gallery than he began gasping for breath. He raced down the stairs and out of the building, where he became violently ill.

Alan stayed away from the museum for two months claiming illness. When he returned, he was just as determined as ever to prove the Gallery had no ghosts. This time he was able to go only a short way up the stairs when he began gagging again. Scarcely able to catch his breath, he fled the building. Ghosts or no ghosts, Alan had finally had enough. He quit the job and never went back.

But the most terrifying example of the ghostly power in the Discovery Gallery took place the afternoon three schoolgirls drifted into it. When they came to the model cell, two of the girls pushed the third girl inside as a practical joke. They slammed the door shut on her and bolted it.

What followed, according to officials and visitors who were there, was an explosion of supernatural fury. With a roar, something like a great whirlwind came sweeping through, rattling doors and windows, snatching papers from tables and desks and sending them careening around the room. Through all this weird commotion came the ghastly screams of the hysterical girl in the cell.

Finally someone made it to the wooden door, slid back the bolt and led the girl out. At that moment the whirlwind died down. Doors and windows stopped rattling. Papers settled on the floor. Calm returned, but not to the girl. Sobbing and shaking uncontrollably, she tried to tell what had happened to her. But her voice came out a jumble of unintelligible words. It was her eyes, glassy with horror, that revealed something of what she had experienced, cooped up in that tiny cell with the raging ghost of a long-dead madman.

12. THE SPECTRES

Mothman

Strange things sometimes happen that can turn a simple little event into a nightmare. On November 16, 1966, around 9 P.M., Mr. and Mrs. Raymond Wamsley invited their friend Marcella Bennett and her two-year-old daughter Tina to join them in a surprise visit to their friends the Thomases.

The Wamsleys lived in a little town in the West Virginia countryside. Ralph Thomas lived up the road in the midst of woodlands.

The Wamsley party drove down the dirt road towards their destination. On the way they had to pass an area formerly used by the army for storing explosives. The cement domes, or igloos, built to contain the explosives, were abandoned. They stood empty. The deserted place had an eerie feel about it. And as the Wamsleys drove by, they noticed a strange red light hovering over one of the igloos. Not having any idea what it was, Richard Wamsley stepped on the gas and sped away. Soon after, they reached the Thomas house, and parked in front.

Marcella Bennett was the first to jump out of the car, carrying her sleeping daughter. At that instant, a figure began to rise slowly behind the car. Marcella thought it must have been lying on the ground when it was disturbed by their arrival. Unable to move, she stared at it as it loomed before her. It was in the shape of a man, huge and grey with great wings folded on its back. And its large red eyes glowed in the dark.

Marcella collapsed, dropping her child, who screamed in pain and terror. The Wamsleys were as terrified as Marcella. They jumped out of the car and raced for the

Thomas house. Behind them Marcella broke through the spell that she was under, snatched up Tina and rushed after them. They were let into the house by three of the Thomas children, who said their parents weren't home.

Ralph Wamsley locked the door behind them and made for the telephone. Excited by the hysteria of the older people, the children rushed to the window and looked out. They saw the strange grey monster shuffling onto the porch.

By the time the police arrived, the creature had disappeared. However, the Mothman, as it came to be called by the press, continued to make numerous appearances elsewhere in West Virginia. Throughout November, witnesses in five counties phoned law enforcement agencies to report sightings of the Mothman.

Richard West, who lived in Charleston, West Virginia, phoned on the evening of November 21 to describe a "Batman" that was sitting on the roof of a neighbor's home. The Batman, he said, must have been six feet (1.8m) tall, with a wing span of some six to eight feet (1.8-2.4m). Besides its great wings, the most distinguishing thing about it was its pair of huge red eyes.

On November 25, Thomas Ury, who was driving along Route 62 about 7:15 in the morning, phoned in to tell about a tall grey man standing in a nearby field. As he watched, the "man" spread a pair of huge wings and flew straight up like a helicopter. When it was about 150 feet (45m) above Ury's car, it began to circle over it. Ury, driving at 75 miles (120km) per hour could not shake the creature. He sped towards the only protection he could think of—Sheriff George Johnson at Point Pleasant. By the time he got there, the Mothman was gone. But Ury was so unnerved, he couldn't go to work that day.

On the evening of November 26, Mrs. Ruth Foster of St. Albans, West Virginia, phoned to say that the Mothman was standing on her front lawn beside the porch. It was tall and had a pinched face that didn't seem to have any other features except for huge red eyes that seemed to pop out of its head like the eyes of a crab.

At 10:30 on the Sunday morning of November 27, 18-year-old Connie Carpenter, who was driving home from church, came face to face with the Mothman, which almost caused her to have an accident.

That evening the Mothman returned to St. Albans and chased two young girls, 13-year-old Sheila Cain and her little sister, as they ran screaming for home.

These were only a few of the calls phoned in to law enforcement agencies about the Mothman. More than 100 were received by the time the month came to an end.

What was this Mothman? Where had it come from? People began putting forward all kinds of explanations. Perhaps the Mothman was a bird from prehistoric times.

Perhaps it was some lost, now almost extinct, species of human being or a mutation caused by gases escaping from the isolated explosives area where it may have been making its home.

Scientists would have loved to examine that strange and terrifying creature. But they never got a chance. As suddenly as it had appeared, the Mothman disappeared, leaving behind no footprints, no droppings, no signs of its visit—only questions.

The Ghosts of
Creek Road

Dark, lonely roads seem to attract ghosts. People claim to have seen a number of them along Creek Road, which winds through the wilderness outside the town of Ohai in Southern California. The road is spooky even in daylight with the interlocking branches of gnarled live oaks overshadowing it. It can be an eerie place after dark. That's when the ghosts come out.

The best known among them is the Charman. Nobody knows his real name. He's called Charman because his body is practically burned to a crisp. Those who have seen him say he's a horrible sight, with flesh peeling away from his bones. His blackened face is a grinning skull from which a few shreds of skin still hang. Some people claim that when he appears he brings with him the sweet stench of burning flesh.

The Charman's anger and pain seem to have accompanied him into death. He has a habit of lunging out of the darkness and attacking anyone walking alone down the quiet road. In 1950 a teenager went for a walk on Creek Road to prove his bravery and came rushing away white-faced, claiming that the Charman had torn his jacket from his back. His story made the papers.

There have been many theories about who the Charman really was. At first people thought he was a fireman who had burned to death in the 1948 fires that raged through the forests surrounding Ohai. Because his body was never found and given a decent burial, he was doomed to walk the shadowy road for all time, taking out his anger on innocent passersby.

This story was disproved when a look at old records showed that no firefighter had been lost in the fire of 1948. Then people said if not a forest fire, an automobile accident must have been the cause of the Charman's fiery death. A few have a much darker theory. They say the Charman could have been the victim of a murderer who torched him and left him to die in the forest. Now filled with rage, he stalks the dark road seeking revenge upon the man who killed him.

The Charman doesn't travel alone on dark, winding Creek Road. A young horsewoman has been seen there on the anniversary of her death. She rides recklessly down Creek Road until she reaches a place called the Curve, which is treacherously sharp. Here the horse stumbles, rears and throws her. She falls, breaks her neck and dies instantly. Then, in the next few minutes, she is back again, riding at breakneck speed to the killer curve. People say that she repeats this ride until day breaks and she can rest for another year.

A third ghost is the young bride who chooses the anniversary of her death to hitchhike down the old road in a white wedding dress stained with blood. No one knows who she was or why she was killed on her wedding day or why she chooses to hitchhike on this spooky road to commemorate the murder.

The fourth ghost in this strange assortment is a motorcyclist. He rides pell-mell down the treacherous road over and over again. It's hard to understand how he negotiates it so skillfully, because, you see, he has no head.

The Black Horse of Sutton

There are stories of phantom horses from all around the world. Usually, these horses are white or black. Sometimes they are never seen—only the clatter of their hooves is heard, along with the rattle of spurs and the smart crack-crack of the whip in the ghostly rider's hands. The horses gallop through history carrying important messages to kings and generals or their ladies.

The Black Horse of Sutton is unique in that it appeared only to a humble woman, old Mrs. Sutton. She and her husband had established a homestead in the bush land outside the town of Goulburn in New South Wales, Australia. It was an isolated place removed many miles from the nearest human settlement. In that general area it was known as the Sutton Homestead, or just plain Sutton.

One spring day, Mr. Sutton had to ride into Goulburn to negotiate a land deal. He left Mrs. Sutton behind on the lonely homestead, promising to return as soon as possible. Those were the days when there were few roads. Transportation depended on the horse. Even the mail might take a month or more to arrive. Mrs. Sutton knew she might have a long wait before her.

Day by day, she waited eagerly for her husband's return. She had no way of knowing when he would be back, except by the sound of the hoofbeats of his returning horse. So one evening, a week after he left, when she heard the distant rat-a-tat-tat of galloping hooves, her heart leapt with happiness. She was sure that her husband was at last on his way home.

Closer and closer came the hoofbeats. They stopped at the outer gate. She heard the horse turning as if the rider were closing the gate behind him. Then came the click of the gate as it closed.

Now the thundering hoofbeats were galloping down the drive and around the corner of the house. Suddenly, a magnificent black stallion came into view. But, to Mrs. Sutton's horror, it was riderless. On hooves that hammered out a staccato beat, the horse galloped directly towards the shuddering woman. She cried out, terrified. But at the last minute the great beast shied away from her and trampled into the house, where it disappeared. The hoofbeats echoed in the ranges of distant mountains. Fainter and fainter they sounded until finally they disappeared altogether.

The next day a messenger arrived to tell Mrs. Sutton that on his way home the evening before, her husband had been thrown by his plodding farm horse. He had been found lying dead by the side of the road while the horse grazed quietly nearby.

Had the black stallion not been riderless after all? Was the soul of Mr. Sutton astride the horse—invisible but still present—as he rode home for the last time?

Twice more the spectre horse appeared to Mrs. Sutton. Once it came to announce the death of her elder son, killed in the Boer War in South Africa. Later, it came to tell her of her younger son's accidental death.

When old Mrs. Sutton died, the homestead she and her husband loved so much was demolished. Progress transformed it into a hamlet of small homes. Fine roads and automobiles linked the inhabitants to the outside world.

And the Black Horse of Sutton gallops no more.

Great Ball of Fire

Diamond Island lies in a river opposite the small hamlet of Hardin, Illinois. Early in 1888 people began talking about a mysterious ball of fire, the size of a large barrel, that appeared around midnight at the foot of the island

and moved around—without, however, setting anything on fire. The light intrigued the people of Hardin so much that they would line the far shore every night to watch it as it drifted here and there before vanishing.

One night a group of young men decided to visit the island and investigate the mysterious light firsthand. Afraid it might be a dangerous smuggler or a thief of some kind, they armed themselves to the teeth for their adventure. Bristling with revolvers, knives, shotguns and clubs, they set out in a small skiff they had rented.

The men were in high spirits as they rowed to the island, landing at a point that was not far from the spot where the light made its nightly appearance. Here they hauled their skiff ashore, beaching it high above the waterline. Then they hid in a grove of trees and waited.

Darkness came down as the hours ticked by. Stars splattered the sky. Nothing unusual was seen or heard above the gentle ripple of the river. Then, just as they were wondering if the whole thing had been a hoax, the light appeared, rising out of the river at the south end of the island.

As it rose, it grew in intensity, flooding the whole area with a crimson light. Higher and higher it went, up, up, up, until it hovered 120 feet (36.5m) in the air. Then it faded away. And darkness seemed to return to the hushed island.

The young men had seen enough. All they wanted now was to escape the island. They rushed for their boat. But as they reached the edge of the shore, they stopped, horrified. The little skiff was already moving out. It seemed to be propelled by the ball of red fire—which was now perched in it!

As the men watched in growing panic, the crimson ball took the shape of a man. He was pulling steadily on the oars, sending the skiff into midstream. His face was hidden under the wide brim of a floppy hat, but the rest of him could be seen quite plainly, because the boat and the waters and air that surrounded him were lit up by the weird brightness.

The young men stood in shocked silence, paralyzed with fear, their eyes fastened on the boat with its ghastly occupant, who was moving farther and farther away. It was as though whoever the spectre was, he was desperately trying to escape the island. But before he could reach the far shore, he changed again into a fiery ball. Slowly it rose from the boat, climbing into the sky, until at treetop level it disappeared. Black night descended once more on the island. Across the river, the lights of Hardin twinkled.

It was as though the young men on the island were released from a binding spell. They began shouting for help at the tops of their voices. At last, a fisherman sleeping on the far shore launched his own boat, pulled across to the island and rescued them.

The fiery ghost continued to make its nightly visits to the island. But neither the young men nor anyone else cared to investigate it again. The people of Hardin were quite willing to accept the only explanation available. Several years before, a man had been betrayed and brutally murdered on the island. The great ball of fire was his restless ghost.

The Expanding Dog

Several years ago, when I visited the Chumash Indian reservation in the Santa Ynez valley, I met an elderly woman known to her friends as Aunt Minnie. She told me about a very strange experience she had had one night when walking home from a visit with a friend.

It was a pleasant summer evening with a young moon riding low in the east. Suddenly, Aunt Minnie heard a whispering sound behind her. At first she thought it was a breeze rustling the leaves of the live oaks. But when she looked up, she saw nothing stirring. She turned around to find out if something was following her. She saw a tiny puppy trotting along behind her.

It didn't look dangerous, but there was something very strange about it. It was no larger than a small matchbox! Whoever heard of a dog that small?

Aunt Minnie quickened her steps, just wanting to get home. But the whispering sound continued to pursue her, and it kept growing louder. She looked back again.

The puppy had grown. It was much larger now, the size of a big cat. A real dog couldn't grow that fast, she thought. Aunt Minnie began to run, but always behind her came the whispering, whispering. She kept glancing over her shoulder—and every time she looked, the dog was bigger, and it was close on her heels.

By the time she reached the gate of her home, the dog was almost as large as a pony and had turned jet black. Huge red eyes glared at her. Fangs gleamed white in slavering, open jaws. Aunt Minnie's knees were so wobbly she could hardly walk. Somehow she managed to push through the gate, stagger to her front door, open it and collapse inside.

Her husband, Ben, helped her to a chair. She sat, pale and shivering, unable to say a word. Ben got a blanket and wrapped her up in it, but she still went on shaking and her teeth were chattering. At last she managed to tell Ben about the dog.

Ben grabbed his gun and ran out to shoot the creature, but it had disappeared. He could hear its faint baying in the hushed night—a ghostly baying that he realized could only come from a ghost dog.

"That's what it was," he told me, "a ghost dog with a ghost shaman for its master. It's been seen by others around here since. We know where it comes from— that old graveyard where the shamans did their black magic.

"No use to shoot at it. I just put my gun away. And told my Minnie she was plenty lucky to get away so quick inside."

13. THE SEARCHERS

The Man in the Bowler Hat

England's Heathrow Airport is noted for its ghosts. Perhaps the most persistent of them is the apparition that appears on Runway No. 1.

It all began back in 1948 when a DC3 Dakota owned by Sabena Belgian Airways tried to make a landing on Runway No. 1 in thick fog and crashed, killing all 22 passengers and crew. The plane burst into flames upon impact.

Airport personnel had just begun sifting through the wreckage when one by one they were interrupted by a man in a dark suit and a bowler hat. He had the same question for everyone:

"Excuse me, have you found my briefcase?"

It was only later at the conference held to determine the cause of the crash that the odd character was noted. Everyone remembered his approaching them with the question and each one thought it rather peculiar. As they discussed it, they began realizing how truly strange it was. The bodies of all the passengers and crew had been identified. None had survived. Then who was the man in the bowler hat?

Some 22 years later, in 1970, this question was asked by a police patrol that was cruising around the airport about one o'clock in the afternoon. A radio call came in, saying that a man in a bowler hat was seen on Runway No. 1. Off raced the police car. But the runway was empty and the police, saying, "False alarm," left. Less than an hour later, they received another call and raced back, only to find the runway still empty. As the afternoon slipped into dusk, the reports of a man in a bowler hat became more frequent. Finally, the control tower got into the act. Something was now appearing on the radar screen—a blip that was moving so slowly it had to be a human being.

This time police and airport personnel were determined to locate the trespasser on Runway No. 1. Three police cars drove side by side down the runway. No way could any human being evade them. Their headlights lit up the runway. It stretched away, empty and silent, before them.

But they had no sooner left the runway than more sightings were phoned in. This time the three police cars were joined by the airport fire engine on which a searchlight was mounted. The next time the control tower picked up the blip on its radar screen, it sent the three police cars and the fire engine racing back to Runway No. 1. Orders came to drive west.

The cars went with doused lights until they were some thirty yards (27m) from the spot where the tower had located the blip. Then they switched on their headlights and searchlight and Runway No. 1 sprang into glaring brightness, empty and silent as before. They inched forward while messages poured in over the radio.

"You're ten yards away now.

"Five yards.

"Four yards.

"Three yards.

"Two yards . . ."

This was followed by a frantic order: "Stop! Whatever it is you've run over it!"

Police and firemen jammed on their brakes and spilled out of the cars and fire engine to look around. Again they found nothing. As before, Runway No. 1 was empty.

A voice crackled over the radio. "You must have missed him. He's walking away from you in the opposite direction. He's behind you now."

The police looked behind them and saw nothing. They drove slowly back. Wearily, they gave up their wild-goose chase, leaving the man in the bowler hat to continue his amble up and down the runway.

What could have been the life and death secret in that lost briefcase that would keep the man in the bowler hat relentlessly searching for it 22 years later?

The Girl from Leigh Park

Outside Waterlooville, England, there's a stretch of road without sidewalks. It's quite dangerous for pedestrians and few are seen on it, especially after nightfall.

On a November evening in 1976, Robert Spensley and his wife, who was at the wheel, were heading for home.

As they reached the dangerous stretch of road, Spensley suddenly saw a girl in the fading light. She was standing directly in the path of the car and his wife was driving straight towards her. He yelled at her to stop or to swerve to miss the girl.

Mrs. Spensley gave her husband a peculiar look and went on driving. Her husband put his hands over his eyes and waited for the thud of impact. There was nothing. When he dared look again, the girl was gone. His wife was still driving calmly. She had seen nothing.

The next morning Spensley reported his strange experience to his co-workers. Several of them spoke up. They had also seen the girl on the road. They said that it was believed to be the ghost of a girl who had once lived in nearby Leigh Park. One evening, while trying to hitch a ride home, she had been struck down by a car and killed. Since that time, she had been seen by a number of motorists on the same stretch of road.

One of Spensley's friends had an even stranger story to tell about the girl from Leigh Park. He said he was driving home through a heavy rain when, as he passed the cemetery, he was flagged down by a young girl. She was wet through, bedraggled and very forlorn. She told him that she lived in Leigh Park and needed a lift there. He opened the door for her and she climbed in. She gave him the address in Leigh Park, but after that little was said by either of them. In the pouring rain, he had to keep his eyes and all his attention on the road. Finally he was in Leigh Park at the address the girl had given him.

"Here we are," he said, bringing the car to a stop. He reached over to open the car door for the girl when, to his shock, he saw that the seat was empty. The girl was gone, though the door was still shut and the window rolled up. For a second, he wondered if she had ever really been there.

Then he looked down at the seat where she had been sitting. It was sopping wet.

The Stuffed Dog

Priory House stands on the Isle of Wight, part of the British Isles. A lovely old house, it is called "Priory" because it was built on the foundations of what was once a Chinese monastery. Something of the peaceful atmosphere of the monastery seems to pervade the old house. Something also haunts it—the ghost of a young girl.

Her portrait hangs in the dining room. It shows a 14- or 15-year-old sitting on a garden seat. She is dressed in a long, blue gown in the style of the early 1700s. A satin ribbon fastens a little canary to her wrist. At her feet lies a small furry dog, a King Charles spaniel. The young girl must have lived in the house at one time, but so long ago that nobody remembers who she was.

Girl and canary have gone to their graves. But the dog remains. Stuffed, he sits in a glass case that is set over the main staircase. From there he surveys the rooms of Priory House with a penetrating stare whenever the light hits his glass eyes.

As for the Little Lady in Blue, as she came to be called, the grave couldn't hold her. She has been seen several times, a faint shadowy figure either on the staircase or in the gardens. She comes with a whiff of lavender perfume, bringing a breath of happiness, a light suggestion of tinkling laughter, the soft swish of silken skirts, and the faint patter of light footsteps as she skips at play.

For many years, the house was occupied by old Miss Laura, who cherished it. Most especially she felt a deep affection for the Little Lady in Blue, that gentle, happy ghost.

Then Miss Laura died. Since she left no heirs, the house was sold by the estate to a wealthy American woman. The new owner poured money into renovations. Most of the old furniture was sold. In its place antiques from different historical periods were bought and the rooms redecorated. The portrait of the Little Lady in Blue stayed. The dog in its glass case went. Finally the American moved in with a large staff of servants and the tranquil atmosphere of the old house was gone.

Now the servants were wakened at night by the sound of a child's feet clattering down the corridors, a child's voice crying between heartrending sobs, "Where is my dog? My little dog, where is he? I want my dog!"

The servants were distracted. One by one, they left. Last to go was the butler, who had worked for the American woman for many years. He told his employer unhappily that he could no longer bear the noises that were setting his nerves on edge.

Something had to be done, but what? Perhaps friends of old Miss Laura would know the answer. The American invited two of them for tea one day and plied them with questions. Why was a child racketing through the halls crying for her dog? What dog?

That was when they told her about the little stuffed dog in the glass case, the stuffed dog that was disposed of when the house was sold. Where was it now?

The American woman was nothing if not determined. She sent out tracers for the little dog, leaving no clue unchecked. Finally she found it in an antique shop in a town miles away. She bought it and returned it to its place above the stairwell. With its return, the noises stopped. Once more there was only the occasional patter of happy feet, a child's light tinkle of laughter, the soft swish of silk passing down the halls, contented sounds that troubled no one.

The American woman has long since sold the Priory. It was bought by a travel organization that had no trouble booking guests who were attracted by the Priory's quaint loveliness, its tranquil atmosphere and, most especially, by the stories of the happy little ghost. Hundreds passed through the old house.

Now and then management changed. But each manager who arrived to take over the job was given a stern warning:

"Whatever else you do, if you want to keep the peace here, never, never remove the stuffed dog in the glass case from its spot over the stairwell."

Where Is My Daughter?

One of the saddest ghosts I've heard of was that of an elderly woman. Back in the 1800s she and her husband had come from Ireland to Australia, where they settled on the west coast near the town of Fremantle. Widowed early, the woman had a beautiful young daughter with red hair and a sweet Irish face. One day her daughter was abducted.

The mother searched for the lost girl frantically until, wild with grief, she went insane and was locked up in the gloomy buildings that made up the asylum at Fremantle. She wandered the halls of her prison hospital, still searching. Then one day she ended her life by throwing herself out of a first-story window that was more than ten feet (3m) above the rocky ground. But her spirit still could not rest. Even after the asylum buildings were renovated to house a museum and an adjacent art center, the old woman continued to haunt their halls, searching for her lost daughter.

A number of people have come face to face with her—a frail wraith that vanished before their eyes. She always wore the same thing—a plain black dress with a white collar and lace frills down the front. A delicate Victorian-style cap framed her face.

Museum employees working late at night reported seeing her, lit by the ghostly lantern she carried, gliding noiselessly through the darkened corridors. And teachers grading papers late at night in their school rooms at the local high school would look down to see a flickering light moving from window to window of the old buildings. And they would whisper to one another that the poor woman was walking again.

Then, on March 19, 1980, Shelley, a young college student, came to the asylum to fulfill an assignment for her photography class. She was to shoot the various rooms of the art center. In one room, trying for an interesting shot, she turned her camera towards the windows. Through the lens she saw, peering back at her, the demented face of an elderly woman in a lace cap. The window in which the face appeared was more than ten feet (3m) above ground level—too high for anyone to play such an elaborate hoax.

Shelley thought at first it might have been just her imagination. But when she had the film developed, there was the face, just as she had seen it through her camera lens.

Shelley's photo was published in the local newspaper and created quite a stir. Photographers of all kinds flocked to the art center in hopes of capturing the old woman's image on film again. None were successful.

In the years that followed, the old woman's wispy figure was no longer seen in the halls of the old asylum. At night the windows were no longer illuminated by the flickering light of her lantern. Why?

Could it be that, looking through the window into the face of the girl behind the camera, she thought she had found her long-lost daughter at last? For Shelley is an Irish girl with beautiful red hair and dancing Irish eyes.

14. THE VIOLENT ONES

The Evil in Room 310

Marsha Bennett told me this story herself. She had been north to visit friends in the state of Washington. Now she was driving back to her home in California. The last lap of the day's journey was over the Cascade range that stretches from Washington to California. It was late evening and snow had begun to fall before she finally reached the little Oregon town where she planned to spend the night.

Tired and ready for a hot meal and a good night's sleep, she stopped at the first place she came upon. It was an old hotel on the main street. The lobby had a musty odor. The seedy clerk behind the desk signed her in. Her room was on the third floor—Room 310. An elderly bellhop helped her with her luggage.

As soon as the door was opened, a blast of hot air struck Marsha full in the face. With the hot air came something else, something she could not define but that filled her with dread. It was heavy and depressing, she explained, "with the strong scent of evil." She felt as if she was about to faint.

All she said was, "It's awfully hot."

The bellhop tinkered with the radiator knobs. Then he opened the window and left. The room began to cool off, but the feeling of despair and dread grew stronger. It centered on the open square of black window space. The terror seemed to speak in her mind.

"Go to the window," it said. "Throw yourself out, out out!"

Terrified, Marsha flung herself on the bed farthest from the window.

"I kept saying no, no, no to that voice," she told me, "but the voice kept insisting."

"You can't fight me, you puny thing," it said. "Sooner or later you'll jump. I'll make you! Jump! Jump! Jump!"

At last Marsha could stand it no longer. She jumped up, calling herself a coward.

"Coward or not," she explained, "I was sure that if I stayed the night, I'd be dead by morning."

Marsha was prepared to sacrifice the money she'd already paid just to leave, but when she went downstairs with her baggage to check out, the clerk never asked what was wrong or if she wished to try another room. He returned the full cash amount to her.

Marsha drove down the street to a modern motel. As she entered the lobby, she felt the dark depression slip from her shoulders. She became almost giddy with relief She had planned to be on her way early the next morning. Instead she decided to stay over a day and look into the history of the old hotel to see if she could discover the reason for her terrifying experience there.

She visited the local library to make a few inquiries. An elderly librarian sat behind the desk.

"I'm just wondering," Marsha said tentatively. "Did anything shocking ever happen in the old hotel?"

The librarian looked at her strangely. "How did you come upon that bit of history?" she asked. "It took the hotel a long time to squash the story."

The librarian went on to tell what had happened. One evening back in 1948 a couple checked into the hotel as Mr. and Mrs. Oscar Smith. The next morning hotel employees found the young woman's body lying on the sidewalk outside the hotel beneath Room 310. The man who had registered as her husband had disappeared.

"At first it was ruled suicide," the librarian concluded. "But then they pried open her fist and found it clutched a handful of dark curly hair, not her own. So they made a search for the murderer. But he was never found . . .

"By the way," the librarian suddenly added, "isn't that a coincidence! It all happened on November 5th, 40 years ago yesterday."

Gas Brackets

Eileen Nye, who has since moved to Australia, tells this frightening story of an incident that took place during her days in England. When her work took her to a small English village, Eileen was delighted. It was quiet and peaceful, a perfect place in which to bring up her eight-year-old daughter.

Eileen found a delightful old gabled house, rented it at once and moved in with her daughter. She chose a charming little room for the child. Though it now had electric lights, it once had been lighted by gas. The old brass brackets still decorated its walls, adding a quaint old-fashioned touch to the room.

Mother and daughter settled into their new home, adjusting easily to the village life. There was just one flaw. A few days after they moved in, the little girl began complaining of a sore throat.

Then one night Eileen woke up to muffled screams coming from her daughter's room. She rushed in and found the child sitting upright in bed, clutching her throat with one hand and pointing with the other to something in the corner of the room. Eileen couldn't see anything there. When the child tried to explain, only garbled sounds came out.

The next day Eileen took the little girl to the village doctor, who couldn't find anything physically wrong, except for one peculiar fact: there were marks on her throat that looked like thumb prints.

That night, something told Eileen to check on her daughter, though she had heard nothing. When she went into the room, the child seemed to be sleeping peacefully. But there was something strange that made Eileen come to the bedside to get a closer look. The little girl's eyes were wide open. She wasn't sleeping— she was unconscious!

Eileen rushed her daughter to the doctor, who admitted the child to a nearby hospital for treatment and observation. Perhaps, he suggested to Eileen, the key to the child's condition might not lie in a physical ailment but in the past of the old house. Why not check into its history?

Eileen followed his advice. She was horrified to discover that a former tenant, now dead, had strangled his wife in the bedroom Eileen's daughter was using. He had then hung the body from one of the brass brackets, perhaps to make it look like a suicide.

Eileen moved out of the house at once and her daughter recovered completely. But the village doctor believes she had a narrow escape in the old house. It's his opinion that if she had stayed in that room another night, she would surely have died at the ghostly hands of a dead strangler.

Vicious Knots

One day in 1928 Mrs. Sims went to visit her family, who lived in Montreal, Canada. The family consisted of her parents, two older sisters, two younger brothers and a beautiful teenage sister. When Mrs. Sims arrived, she found something strange was going on.

Knots were appearing mysteriously throughout the house.

There were knots in the window curtains and knots in the clothes hanging in the closets. The knots had first appeared in a back room where the teenager stayed. From there they had spread to other downstairs rooms. Then they began appearing upstairs. Soon knots showed up in the mother's best dresses. They were tied so tightly that many of her clothes were ruined. Mrs. Sims decided to stay and help her family through this strange crisis.

As the days passed, more and more peculiar things began to happen. One night, when Mrs. Sims and her parents were in the house alone, they started walking down the long hall to the living room when they stopped short. The thick drapes that usually hung in the hallway had been gathered up and tied together. Several heavy overcoats had been woven into them to form a gigantic tangled knot that hung three feet above the floor. An umbrella thrust into the knot pointed skyward like an exclamation point. Mrs. Sims gasped and then ran screaming from the house. It was several hours before she found the courage to return.

Two days later, something even more frightening happened. Mrs. Sims' mother woke in the middle of the night to find that the top blanket had been ripped off her bed and tied in a huge knot. It hung directly over her face, as if it were preparing to smother her. It seemed that the knots were becoming deadly now.

By this time, word of the knots was spreading. Visitors began flocking to the house—Spiritualists, reporters, two detectives from the police department. The detectives searched the house. They found a foul stench in the basement—a stench the family said they had never smelled before. Bloodhounds were brought in to sniff out a possible murder victim. No victim was found.

Finally, the detectives asked each person in the family to tie a knot. The youngest daughter was the only one to tie the intricate kind of knot that had been appearing all over the house. It seemed as though she was the one responsible. But, if so, how could she have done it when even muscular adults couldn't have handled those heavy drapes in the hall? And how could she have made the knots appear when she wasn't even home?

The knot-tying went on for six weeks. Then one day the teenager summoned her mother and one of her older sisters to her room. As the door opened to let them in, Mrs. Sims saw the curtains blowing wildly— though the windows were closed. The room itself seemed to brim with an eerie force.

Mrs. Sims waited outside the room for what seemed like a long while. Finally, her mother came out. Her grim face was white and her eyes were sick with horror and fear. But she never said a word. Neither she nor her daughters ever spoke about what took place in that room that day, when she grappled with the force that had been terrorizing the household. However, from then on, the knot-tying stopped and the family returned to its former normal routines.

What price did Mrs. Sims' mother have to pay when she bartered for the peace of her family in that closed-off room? Only three people know the answer to that.

Evil Hands

During the time that Amanda was a member of the staff on Quarantine Station, she often said she wasn't afraid of the ghosts that people claimed to have seen there. She wasn't afraid, that is, until the night one tried to kill her.

Back in Colonial times, the Station was established on the rocky North Point of Manly Peninsula, a suburb of Sydney, Australia. When epidemics broke out on ships bringing immigrants to Australia, everyone aboard was quarantined at Manly Cove until the danger of contagion was past. Few survived the quarantine period.

Today Quarantine Station is a national park. The old whitewashed buildings used as hospital and isolation wards have been preserved as landmarks. But something else seems to have survived, too—the ghosts of those who died here. So many sightings have been reported that guides regularly conduct ghost tours through the sprawling grounds.

Whether anyone sees a ghost or not, almost everyone admits to feeling the eerie atmosphere that settles upon Quarantine Station after dark. The spell is so strong that even members of the staff make sure to leave with the last tour group every night.

Only Amanda chose to remain. She couldn't imagine why anyone should fear the spirits of the gentle, suffering settlers who were buried here, and she loved the lonely beauty of the grounds. She was so confident of her safety that she made one of the isolation wards her living quarters, spending nights as well as days in it.

Then, one horrifying night of bright moonlight, everything changed. Amanda went for a walk along the coastal cliffs that fall away from the headlands on which Quarantine Station stands. She lingered there, revelling in the silence, gazing across the dark harbor at the lights of Sydney, as the moonlight spread its mysterious web over the dreaming land and sea.

All at once her mood was shattered. A presence hot and evil seemed to be pressing close against her. Strong hands suddenly struck her in the middle of her back. They began shoving her forward with tremendous force.

Amanda's feet scrabbled on the rocky cliff edge as she fought to regain her balance. Far below she could see the white line of surf breaking silver against the rocks. She knew that if she went down she would be bashed to death on those rocks. She had to get free. But no matter how hard she struggled, she couldn't break away from the thing that was pushing her so relentlessly forward.

Now her feet were beginning to slide over the brink. Pebbles were being dislodged. She could hear the clattering of the stones on the rocks below and knew she was about to follow them. She was down to her last chance.

Gathering up all the strength she had, Amanda flung herself backwards. The cruel hands loosened, their force spent. Amanda whirled around to see who was there. There was nothing! Everything was quiet and hushed as before.

Terrified, Amanda fled back along the footpath that had seemed so friendly only minutes before. She stumbled and fell and got up again and ran, gasping, all the way until she reached the safety—would it ever be safe again?—of the isolation ward.

Early the next day she resigned from her job and left Quarantine Station forever. Those invisible, cruel hands had reminded her of something she had forgotten. The first shipload of passengers to be detained at Quarantine Station had been convicts—and some among them had been violent criminals.

15. THE GUARDIANS

A Call for Help

Seventeen-year-old Liv Ullmann was in London for the first time. The beautiful Norwegian actress had spent most of her childhood in the little town of Trondhage, Norway. Her widowed mother supported herself and her child with the proceeds from a small dress shop she owned.

From the time she was small, Liv had always wanted to be an actress. When she reached her 17th birthday, her mother sent her to London to study drama under actress Irene Brent. Liv stayed at the London Y.W.C.A. Outside the security of that rooming house, London glittered with fascinating sights. The girl saw nothing there to threaten her, for she judged the big city by the experiences she had had in her hometown, where everyone was always friendly and everyone—even strangers—could be trusted.

One afternoon, about five o'clock, Liv and a friend were walking along a London street when a limousine slowed and then stopped beside them. A kindly-looking, well-dressed man leaned out the car window and asked the girls if they wanted a ride home.

Back in Norway, they had often accepted rides from fellow Norwegians whom they didn't know. So they climbed into the limousine without thinking. As soon as they were in the back seat, the man pushed a switch that locked all the doors automatically. He also shut and locked the sliding glass window that separated him from the girls. They found themselves in a tight little prison from which there was no escape.

Too late Liv remembered the stories she'd read in the

London newspapers about girls who were kidnapped to be sold into slavery in foreign lands. Terrified, the teenagers struggled to open the doors. They pounded on the glass window that separated them from the driver. The man in the front seat paid no attention to their struggles and screams.

Finally, Liv stopped struggling and began to pray. She thought of her mother in faraway Norway, her mother who had always been there to protect her. She folded her hands and sent out a silent plea.

"Mother, mother," she whispered, "Help! Help me!"

Shortly afterwards, the car slowed down.

The girls held their breath.

The man in the front seat slid back the window that separated him from the girls.

'Where do you live?" he asked.

When they told him, he drove to the Y.W.C.A., unlocked the doors and swung them open. As the girls scrambled out, he said, "Well, maybe you've learned a lesson."

It seemed to the teenagers that they had been in that terrible car for ages. But when Liv looked at her watch, she was surprised to see how little time had gone by. It was only five minutes past five.

The next week Liv got a letter from her mother.

"Please tell me what you were doing last Wednesday afternoon," her mother wrote. "I was in the shop when suddenly an overwhelming fear for you forced me to go to the back room. There I fell to my knees and I folded my hands and I prayed for your life and your safety as I have never prayed before. It was just five minutes past five when I felt the dark cloud lift and I could go back to work."

Liv says her mother never had had a psychic experience before. But the bond between them is so strong that she was able to pick up her daughter's desperate cry for help. Liv is sure that it was her mother's fervent prayer fueled by love that was able to soften the mind of a hardened criminal many miles away.

Footsteps

A practical nurse, Phyllis Hudson has met a lot of odd people in very unusual circumstances. One of the strangest cases occurred in an old house in Westcott, near Darling, England.

The house stood in the center of what was once a rose garden, the pride of the neighborhood. The bushes, tended by the owner of the house, had been covered with luxuriant blooms. But since he died two years before, the garden had grown to weeds and it was too much for his widow to handle.

When the widow herself became seriously ill and was confined to bed, she required 24-hour care, so Mrs. Hudson was hired as a live-in nurse.

The widow's bedroom was on the second floor of the rambling two-story house. At first Mrs. Hudson slept in a small bedroom next to her charge. But she soon changed to a room at the opposite end of the house. The reason Mrs. Hudson changed rooms also kept relatives away from night visits to the widow. After seven P.M. no one came to see her, no matter how many might arrive during daylight hours.

The reason was the footsteps. At ten o'clock every night footsteps would be heard at the front door. Slowly, deliberately, they would cross the hall to the stairs and then start mounting them steadily.

At first, Mrs. Hudson thought it was an intruder. She stood at the head of the stairs and watched anxiously. But though she could hear the footsteps mounting higher and higher, she saw no one. She might have laid it all down to imagination, except for the family dog. When the footsteps started climbing upwards he would sit beside her at the top of the stairs, cowering, the thick ruff of hair on the back of his neck standing upright, a growl deep in his throat. He was obviously terrified.

As the footsteps came towards her, Mrs. Hudson could no longer stand her ground. She would back away from the stairs and hurry down the hall to her own room. With a final yap, the dog would follow her, tail between his legs.

The footsteps would reach the upper landing and go into the widow's bedroom. The only one not upset by the footsteps was the old woman herself, who said the invisible visitor was just her husband coming to make his nightly call.

One day the widow died, and from that moment the footsteps no longer sounded in the silent house. But to everyone's amazement, the dilapidated rose garden suddenly burst into huge fragrant blossoms more beautiful than anyone could remember having seen before.

People around there said it was the husband's way of giving his wife a royal welcome.

Dreamtime Visitor

An Aboriginal family living in a small town in South Australia went on a camping trip in the Coorong. The Coorong is a coastal strip of swamp and dunes about

87 miles (140km) long. Low tide along the Coorong exposes wide expanses of salt flats. That night the Aboriginal family was out spotlighting on the flats. To spotlight, they shone their powerful hand-held flashlights across the flats to pick up crabs and other sea creatures.

All at once, the powerful lights illuminated a trail of giant footprints crossing the muck. They were spaced about four feet (1.2m) apart. The Aborigines looked out over the flats to see what had made the tracks, and found themselves staring into two shining eyes the size of automobile headlights, and they were spaced almost the same distance apart. But their eerie sheen was unlike any car lights the Aborigines had ever seen. As they looked into the huge eyes, the terrified family felt a strange tingling sensation travelling through their bodies, like an electric charge. They turned and fled.

At first the non-Aboriginal neighbors of the family scoffed at the story, calling it a wild fairy tale. Then some of those neighbors went camping on the Coorong and saw for themselves the great eyes staring at them and felt the same electric chill of fear. Other reports began to filter in.

One came from Cooberpedy, some 700 miles (1127 km) to the north of the Coorong. Cooberpedy is a little opal-mining town in Australia's inland desert region where rainfall averages less than three inches (8cm) a year. Only the hardiest desert growths can exist there. Most large creatures would find it difficult to survive.

There aren't many homes above ground in Cooberpedy. People use bulldozers to dig cave homes in the low hills that surround the town. These homes are beautifully furnished and quite comfortable. Josh and his family live in one of them. Sometimes he and his neighbors get together for an evening of bridge.

One night the bridge players were gathered in Josh's home, a game in progress. Suddenly Josh felt a tingling like a strong electric charge run through his body. The hair on his arms stood up. His scalp crawled. He jumped to his feet and ran to the front door. Flinging it open, he stepped outside.

The sky above him was velvet black, sparkling with desert stars against which the humps of hills rose in scallops. Then he turned to see two great luminous eyes staring down upon him from the summit of the hill at whose base he stood. The eyes were set about four feet (1.2m) apart, and there was a strange glitter in them. Josh had seen that glow before. It was the same glitter that appeared in the eyes of his cat when it was stalking a mouse.

Shaking with terror, Josh slammed the door shut and told his neighbors what he had seen. But, by the time they rushed out to get a look at the eyes, the creature had disappeared.

What animal has such huge, piercing eyes? None in this world that we know of, that's certain. But the Aborigines have an answer.

"They're our animal ancestors, the dreamtime heroes," they explain. "We use secret rituals to enter the dreamtime in which they still live. So why can't they leave the dreamtime to visit us? And when they do, better watch out. Some of those fellas can be pretty fierce and mean, if you make them mad."

The Fourth Presence

When Sir Ernest Shackleton wrote a book about his experiences in Antarctica, he mentioned a Fourth Presence that had once saved his life. It began in 1914 when Shackleton embarked on an ambitious plan to cross Antarctica by way of the South Pole.

The expedition, the second he had made to the frozen continent, was jinxed from the start. He had hoped that the Weddell Sea off the coast of Antarctica would be navigable. Instead, unseasonable weather had broken up the firm sheet of ice that usually, at this time of year, lined the coast. Now smaller sheets of ice (ice floes) of all shapes and sizes along with icebergs filled the bay. They crashed and ground against each other as storms roiled the waters below. Shackleton's ship was imprisoned in this churning jumble of ice blocks, and then it was crushed. On November 21st, it sank, leaving the 28-man crew to survive as best it could on the ice floes.

It was the following April before there was sufficient open water to launch the three small boats the men had brought with them from their sinking ship. On these boats they made their way to isolated Elephant Island, which provided shelter, but little else. There was no chance of rescue from the island because ships bypassed it.

Shackleton decided to make his way to the island of South Georgia, where there was a large whaling station. Two of the three boats were too small to make the more than 800-mile (1280km) journey there. Shackleton chose six men to accompany him in the largest boat.

It took 16 days for them to reach King Haakon Bay on South Georgia. Enclosed by tall, rugged cliffs, the harbor was almost as isolated as Elephant Island. The men would have to get to the opposite side of South Georgia, where the whaling station was located.

The boat in which they had come was so battered by storms and high seas that Shackleton was afraid it would never make the trip. Land passage was the only way, even though he knew the interior of the island was a gigantic death trap. No one had ever been able to cross it before.

Shackleton chose two able men, Worsley and Crean, to accompany him. They planned to travel light, taking only three days' rations, a primus lamp filled with oil, a small cooker, a few matches, an adze that could be used as an ice axe, and a 50-foot (15m) long alpine rope. Though it was bitter cold, they left their sleeping bags behind, because the weight would have slowed them down.

The trio set out at three o'clock in the morning. The sky was clear with a full moon shining. By its light the men threaded a path around the glacier that spilled down the cliffs into Haakon Bay. It took them two hours to climb 2500 feet (962m). From there they could look out on a mass of high peaks fronted by perpendicular cliffs. Steep snow slopes fell away in all directions. The frozen rivers of ancient glaciers glimmered in the moonlight.

Swallowing their fear, the men set off through the forbidding, frigid world. As they tramped through soft snow, Shackleton suddenly felt a fourth presence, invisible but real, walking at his side. During the long, harrowing trek, the presence stayed with him. It was there when blinding fogs blanketed everything. It seemed to give him strength as, dangling from the rope, he chiselled steps in a glacier's steep slope for the men to follow. It built up his resolve when, time after time, he found himself going in the wrong direction and had to lead his men back along the hazardous way they had come. It was there, too, a protector and guide, as the three picked their way through mazes of dangerous crevasses, half concealed by snow.

On the second night, exhausted, half frozen, despairing, the men had to force themselves to trudge on under the cold moon. They didn't dare stop for sleep, because without their warm bags, sleep would end in death. Through the long hours, the presence continued to stay with them, lending courage and strength.

Finally, 36 hours after they had set out from King Haakon Bay, the men achieved the impossible. They reached the shore and the whaling station without any loss of life or serious injury. Never once had Shackleton mentioned the presence during the long trek. Perhaps he was afraid his men might think he had lost his mind.

But to his amazement, Worsley broke the silence.

"Boss," he said, "you know, I had a curious feeling on the march there was another person with us."

Quickly, Crean agreed. He had felt it too and been comforted and encouraged by it. But, like Shackleton, neither man had voiced his feelings aloud until that moment.

What could it have been that walked with Shackleton and his men during the hours they faced death in the lonely, tumbled wastes of a frozen island? Who was the Fourth Presence?

16. CURSES AND VENGEANCE

When Death Comes on Swift Wings

It was a warm evening in April, 1924, and the three young men were enjoying a card game on the deck of the steamer as it sailed lazily down the River Nile.

They had not met until the voyage started, but they had so many interests in common that they were soon firm friends.

Gordon Richardson, 26, was an archaeologist whose

main interest was exploring the tombs of the pharaohs. After the card game, he amused his friends, Ian Grant and Philip Masters, by talking about some of his experiences. Masters jokingly mentioned the ancient curse of the pharaohs: "Death shall come on swift wings to him that defileth the tomb of a pharaoh." Wasn't Richardson worried about that? he teased. Richardson laughed and explained that he kept an open mind on these matters.

The next morning, the steamer arrived at Aswan and the trio wandered ashore to the market, where Grant was intrigued by a mummy case that an Arab trader was selling. Grant had beaten the Arab down from the equivalent of $100 to $80, when Richardson took over, speaking in rapid Arabic. Minutes later, he told the others that the price was down to $32.

As the mummy case was genuine and would easily fetch $450 in London, Richardson suggested that each of them put up $8. It would add a little spice to their card games if ownership of the mummy went to whichever one was the winner when the journey ended in Cairo.

The mummy case was taken aboard and maneuvered into the nearest cabin, Grant's.

The next morning, Grant did not turn up as usual for breakfast. When the steward went to his cabin, the only occupant was the mummy case standing unseeing in the corner.

Grant's bunk had not been slept in, and he was never heard of again. He was presumed to have fallen overboard and been drowned, but no cry for help had been heard.

Richardson and Masters were stunned by the tragedy. That evening, Richardson retired early to his cabin, where the case had been taken. When he failed to appear for breakfast the following morning, Masters went to his cabin anxiously. Richardson was in bed, but only semiconscious and suffering from fever. A few hours later he was dead. A post-mortem was carried out, but the cause of his death remained a mystery.

Masters refused pointblank to have the mummy case in his cabin, because he could not believe that the double tragedy was a coincidence. When he disembarked in Cairo, a cable was waiting to inform him that the family business had been ruined in a bank crash.

When the mummy case arrived in England, it was promptly sold, yet its history of tragedy was by no means over. Some years later, Madame Blavatsky, a celebrated clairvoyant, was invited to a large party in London. She had no sooner arrived than she announced that she was quite unable to stay in the house and had to leave immediately. There was some malevolent influence there, she said—something diabolical and harmful.

A little annoyed, the host jokingly invited her to have

a look around and locate the ghost for them. Madame Blavatsky went into all the rooms without comment, but on entering the attic, she stiffened and exclaimed, "It is here. I feel it!"

She hunted around the room in semi-darkness, opened a closet in the far corner and found the mummy case. The owner of the house looked at it in astonishment. She had never seen it before as she only bought the house a week earlier, after the sudden death of the previous tenants. Madame Blavatsky had never been inside the house before or heard the history of the mummy case, but she left at once, imploring her hosts to get rid of the evil thing immediately.

Her advice was taken and the mummy case was given to the British Museum, where two porters carried it upstairs. One fell on the steps and broke his leg; the other died suddenly of a heart attack the following day.

Dr. Budge, in charge of the mummy, had a photographer take pictures of the object for a catalogue. The next day the photographer rushed out of the darkroom in great excitement to tell a fellow technician that there was something extraordinary about the photograph.

His colleague shuddered when he examined the negative beneath a light, for there was no doubt about it; there *was* a macabre-looking face leering, somehow, through the mummy case.

As there wasn't time that day to make prints, the photographer dropped in to see Dr. Budge on his way home, to tell him about the phenomenon. Budge was most anxious to see a print of the picture, so the photographer returned to his studio to make it up. That was the last time he was seen alive.

The following morning, his colleagues found the darkroom door locked from the inside. Forcing it open they found the photographer lying dead on the floor, with a cruel gash across his throat.

There was no sign of the negative or any prints that involved the mummy case. Neither was there any weapon that could have been used in the suicide—or murder.

The Witch Doctor of Pulo Jehat

The island had lain undisturbed for 100 years. Like a sentinel, it rose up from the waters of the Johore Straits, the narrow strip of sea that separates Singapore from the Malayan mainland. The natives called it Pulo Jehat—the Wicked Island.

243

Over the years, few had dared to set foot on it. It was cursed, they said, and protected by an evil, all-powerful guardian named Merah, who had been dead for more than a century.

A powerful witch doctor, Merah had lived alone in the middle of a mangrove swamp on what is now Singapore Island. Since, according to Malayan folklore, evil spirits are unable to cross water, when Merah died, he was buried on the little island at the eastern end of the Johore Straits.

But although Merah was dead, his evil lived on in native legends, even after the village grew into the great port of Singapore. And in 1938, when the British decided to strengthen the defenses of Singapore against a possible attack from the sea, it became evident just how deeply rooted these local superstitions were.

The British planned to set up a number of guns to guard the eastern approaches to the Johore Straits, and Pulo Jehat was the ideal site. But there was a problem: No native laborers would go near the place. Both Malay and Chinese workmen were convinced that to set foot on Pulo Jehat meant risking Merah's fury. Even an offer of double pay failed to change their minds.

At last, a Muslim priest, who lived on the neighboring island of Tekong, contacted army authorities. He said he might be able to solve the problem by visiting the island

and communing with the spirit of the dead witch doctor. He would try to persuade Merah's ghost to lie low until the gun stations were completed. In view of the fearful dangers involved, he asked a small fee— $100 (£60).

The priest spent two days alone on Pulo Jehat; and when he returned, he told the authorities that Merah had "agreed" not to hinder the army's work, provided that no one disturb his tomb.

Somewhat reassured, the local laborers began work, and after six weeks the gun placements were completed. The job had gone ahead without interference, supernatural or otherwise. The army had its fortifications; the Muslim priest had earned his fee; the workers had earned their double pay. Everyone was happy—until the engineer came along.

He was a representative of the British firm that supplied the power plant for the installation. When the work was finished, he visited the island to make sure that the firm's equipment was in working order.

Even after ten years in the Far East, the engineer was convinced that superstition was a load of nonsense. And despite the entreaties of his Chinese assistant, he was determined to prove it—by spitting on Merah's tomb.

To his assistant's amazement, nothing happened. No winged demons appeared to carry off the engineer; no thunderbolt flashed out of the sky to strike him down.

But things began to go wrong.

A few hours later, one of the engineer's staff, a Chinese mechanic, had the fingers of his right hand sliced off by the fan of a diesel engine's watercooler.

Then the electricity generators on the island stopped working for no apparent reason. The diesel engines that powered them were still running perfectly, and there was nothing to account for the sudden failure.

The next morning the generators hummed to life without a hitch. They continued to work perfectly for another month, and then the power failed again. This time, the fault was traced to the heavy, lead-covered cables that ran across the island from the generator building to the gun positions.

At the exact spot where the cables passed Merah's tomb, their protective lead covering had flaked away like dry clay.

The lead was renewed, and the equipment gave no more trouble. But within a week, the curse of Merah struck again. A piece of equipment fell out of a boat that was being unloaded on Pulo Jehat, and a Malay coolie dived into the sea to recover it.

Seconds later, he was dead—his lower body crushed in the jaws of a shark.

One Japanese pilot tried to bomb the gun positions on

the island. His bomb missed its target, and the gunners below watched as the bomber continued its dive. It was not damaged in any way—yet the pilot seemed frozen at the controls. The plane smacked into the sea and blew up.

The engineer who had spat on Merah's tomb escaped from Singapore just a few hours before the Japanese captured the city. He was lucky—or so it seemed at first.

But three months later, his eyesight began to fail. Eye specialists were completely baffled, but there was nothing they could do. Eventually, he went totally blind.

Since then, Merah has been left to rest in peace.

Curse of the Old Ones

Just north of Mombasa, where the Indian Ocean rolls gently against Kenya's 250-mile-long coastline, lies the ancient city of Gedi. A crumbling ruin, overgrown with creepers, it has been abandoned for centuries. No one knows who lived there, or why they left, and no native will go near the place.

But this is not just because of the snakes and poisonous creeping creatures that infest the city. According to local legend, Gedi is guarded by the "Old Ones"—the spirits of priests who once ruled the temple and promised to protect the ruins throughout eternity. It's easy to believe this legend, because Gedi is veiled by an uncanny silence, and huge trees spread their canopies over the ruins as if to enfold countless dark mysteries.

Some years ago, an English tourist named Jack Bateson was attracted by the legends that surrounded Gedi. As he was something of an artist, he thought that the ruins, particularly the ancient temple, would make a good subject for a painting.

When Bateson told his native guide what he planned to do, the man was horrified and begged him not to go. The Old Ones wrought a terrible vengeance, the guide said, on anyone rash enough to remove anything from their home. And they would surely never forgive anyone taking away an image of their sacred temple in the form of a painting!

Bateson laughed. He didn't believe in spirits, and what harm could there be in painting a picture of what, after all, was nothing more than a crumbling ruin?

The next day he loaded his painting materials and a picnic lunch into his car and set out for Gedi, accompanied by his wife and two daughters.

It turned out to be a splendid day. It was cool beneath

the trees, and Bateson had seldom felt so relaxed. Only once, about three o'clock in the afternoon, did anything strange happen. Bateson was sketching the old temple when he saw—or *thought* he saw—a white-robed figure flitting among the trees. None of the others had seen the apparition, so Bateson shrugged the matter off, dismissing it as a trick of the light. Nevertheless, he couldn't shake off a feeling of unease.

Twilight fell quickly, and suddenly the ruins took on a sinister appearance. Bateson felt a peculiar wave of tiredness sweep over him, and with it came an overpowering urge to flee from the place as quickly as possible.

The feeling vanished as soon as Bateson and his family were on the road back to Mombasa—and, strangely, he found that he was driving in brilliant sunshine. Dusk had touched the ruins long before it crept over the rest of the area!

Still, the time spent at Gedi had been rewarding, because the pictures and sketches were among the best he had ever done. The next day he showed his painting of the ancient temple to a friend, who immediately offered to buy it. Impulsively, Bateson *gave* him the picture as a parting gift, since the Batesons were returning to England in a few days' time.

Back home, immersed in the everyday routine of work, Bateson forgot about Gedi. He didn't give the Old

Ones or the legend a thought—not even when he fell downstairs and broke his leg a few weeks later.

He was hardly on his feet again when there was another accident. This time the victim was his eldest daughter, who broke an ankle playing hockey.

Then his wife slashed her hand badly with a pair of garden shears.

Bateson told himself that these were just unfortunate coincidences. Then a letter arrived from his friend in :Mombasa—the one to whom he had given the painting. To his horror, Bateson learned that his friend's family had experienced a similar catalogue of accidents.

Bateson felt strangely compelled to return to Kenya. As soon as his work permitted, he flew to Mombasa, leaving his family in England and taking his pictures of Gedi with him. The morning after his arrival he was leaving his hotel when he met the native guide who had first warned him not to go to Gedi.

"I knew you would return," the African said. "It is well, for you have very little time. The Old Ones will not wait much longer. There is only one thing to do— you must burn the paintings."

Slowly, Bateson returned to his room. He had made up his mind: the Old Ones had to be appeased. It would break his heart, but he would destroy the paintings.

His sad task completed, Bateson hired a car and

drove to his friend's house. The man greeted him warmly, but looked pale and ill. Bateson urged him to destroy the painting of the ruined temple, which was hanging over the mantelpiece. The man laughed incredulously and flatly refused, saying that the painting was one of his most treasured possessions. Nothing Bateson said or did could change his mind.

Bateson flew back to England. The curse of the Old Ones seemed to have been lifted; he had no more accidents.

Less than a month later, he learned that his friend, together with his entire family, had been killed in a car crash.

The Curse of the Witches of Skye

A cold, wintry gale was howling outside, as Margaret Fraser lay on the couch in front of the peat fire in the cottage where she and her husband, Norman, lived on the west coast of Scotland's Isle of Skye. It was December, 1900.

Margaret was expecting her fourth child, and since

her husband, a shepherd, was out on the hillside, Mrs. Mackinnon, a neighbor, had come in to help tend the youngest of the Frasers' three children, Morag, a little girl about a year old.

Both women were drowsy. Soon Mrs. Mackinnon nodded off, lulled by the warmth of the glowing peat fire.

Margaret Fraser was almost asleep too, when she heard a low muttering. She opened her eyes and saw three ugly little old women sitting around the fire, whispering together, as they admired the sleeping child. They were certainly not women from the neighborhood. Then Margaret suddenly understood: these were no ordinary visitors. They were witches who had come to harm the baby.

Margaret pretended to sleep while one of the hags got up, reached out for the child, and said to the others: "We will take her away and leave at once."

The other two disagreed. "You have so many from this house already," countered one. "Better instead to put a curse on her."

So the first witch cast a spell.

"When this sod of peat shall burn away, that child shall die and go to clay." And she hurled a piece of peat into the fire.

Then the witches vanished. Margaret rose quickly from her couch, took the piece of peat from the fire and extinguished it in a pail of water. Then, wrapping the peat in a rag, she locked it away in a chest and hoped that she had beaten the awful curse.

The chest and its dreadful secret remained a mystery in the family for more than 20 years. Morag, the baby girl, grew up to be a beautiful young woman who eventually became engaged to a handsome young man.

It was the custom in the islands in those days that an engaged girl did not attend church from the day of her betrothal until the day of her marriage.

So one Sunday, while her parents attended church, Morag felt more tempted than ever to have a look in the old chest that her mother always kept locked and hidden in the cupboard.

She found a screwdriver and forced it open. She saw nothing unusual inside, except a piece of charred peat, wrapped in a rag.

She couldn't imagine what possessed her mother to keep a piece of peat so carefully concealed in a chest. She had never heard it spoken of in the family.

Morag could not think of any better use for the piece of peat than to toss it on the fire.

No sooner had the peat begun to burn than the girl grew afraid. She was seized with a strange feeling that something was going to happen to her.

Meanwhile, Morag's parents were making their way

home from church. As they walked they heard an oyster-catcher down by the shore crying, "Kleep-kleep." This bird, when in flight, looks like a black-and-white cross. Its melancholy cry was taken as a warning of imminent disaster.

Getting nearer home, the Frasers heard their dog whining anxiously and saw the animal running around the house, obviously excited. They ran to the cottage.

Inside they found Morag. She was dying from no visible cause. There was no sign of the peat that the witches had cursed more than 20 years before. It had burned to nothing. The fate that Morag had been saved from in her infancy had caught up with her at last.

17. MURDER LIVES ON!

Death in a Dark Mirror

Max Hellier was never able to explain exactly what it was that woke him from his normally deep sleep. He could usually sleep through any disturbance.

The room was pitch-black, and although there was no light of any sort from the window, a faint, bluish glimmer permeated the gloom. It was a weird pulsating reflection of light, unlike any Hellier had ever seen.

Then he noticed that the light was surrounding the reflection of the bedroom door in the mirror on the opposite wall. But it was something else that almost made his heart stop beating. For although he could see nobody beside him in the bed, a quick glance to the side showed a definite indentation of the pillow and the outline of a body beneath the blankets.

Even worse, there was a sudden intense coldness beside him—almost as if he were lying beside a corpse! He glanced in the mirror again and stifled a scream of horror. Hellier couldn't see *himself* reflected in the dark mirror, but there was another man lying there—a burly, bearded, handsome man with a swarthy complexion. And at that instant, Hellier could *hear* the man's heavy breathing.

Then—still in the mirror—he saw the bedroom door open slowly and a woman peer in. Her eyes were fixed on the figure of the bearded man on the bed.

Hellier watched as she crept up to the man with a horrible, feline stealth and gripped the sleeper's throat with her long, bony fingers. He stared silently at the mirror as she squeezed the last breath of life from the hefty man. Then suddenly the hideous drama ended. The picture faded and Hellier was once more alone in the room.

Badly shaken by this experience, Hellier wished he had stayed somewhere else. He had disliked the room in the inn in Munich as soon as he saw it, especially the tall mirror that overshadowed the room, reflecting every movement, every tiny disturbance. Hellier, like many people, never slept on the left side of his bed, and now, as he sat shivering in the huge bed, staring at the empty mirror, he was grateful for his habit of sleeping on the right. He sank thankfully back onto the pillows and tried to blot the dreadful vision of murder from his mind.

In the morning, he was sure that he had either dreamed the incident or else that his tired brain had run riot. He would have left the inn that very day except that he met an old army buddy walking through Munich. Franz Braun was down on his luck. His heart had always been in painting, but Hellier knew he had little talent. Braun had no job, no money, and that very morning had been evicted from his lodgings.

Hellier offered Braun a meal at the inn and a night's lodging—not only out of friendship. Hellier wanted to see if Braun too would see the strange scene in the mirror!

It turned out that now, in 1952, Braun had changed little from his war days. He wined and dined lavishly on Hellier's money and spent the whole evening flirting with the barmaid.

Hellier had already gone up to the room when Braun came bustling in.

"She had to get back to work," he told Hellier, "so we may as well turn in for the night."

Hellier nodded.

Braun said, "The girl warned me not to sleep on the left side of the bed. I wonder why."

Hellier had not told Braun about the apparitions in the mirror, but Braun was skeptical anyway about supernatural experiences. They settled down to sleep, Braun on the left side of the bed.

It was hours later when Hellier woke to find that the room was deadly cold and, in the mirror at the foot of the bed, the bedroom door glowed again with that ghostly light.

He stared at the reflection. There was no sign of himself or Braun in the mirror, but the form of the heavy, dark-skinned man was once more lying on the left-hand side. Hellier turned to look at the form beside him, but the face on the pillow was that of Franz Braun.

Hellier looked back to the mirror, and just as it had on the previous night, the door in the mirror opened slowly. The same gaunt, marble-like face peered in and, with brutish determination, the figure crept towards the bed, its face contorted with malice. The cruel white fingers settled once more on the throat beneath the man's bushy beard.

Hellier watched fascinated as the woman's hands

clasped tighter and tighter. Then, as the shuddering form in the mirror grew still, both figures vanished.

Braun had not stirred at all during the drama, but now Hellier turned to his friend and shook him. Braun could not be roused. Alarmed, Hellier snapped on the light, and then he let out a cry of sheer terror.

Braun was dead. On his throat were two red marks, slowly fading from sight.

Hellier's scream roused everybody. The doctor who was called attributed Braun's death to heart failure, but Hellier knew that Braun had been as healthy as a young horse.

The next day he questioned the barmaid, who had warned Braun about sleeping on the left-hand side of the bed. The girl looked at him uncertainly before saying, "I was right to warn him, Herr Hellier. The last few people who slept on the left side of that bed died in exactly the same way . . ."

Spook House

It had once been known as Spook House, the old building in Hydesville, Massachusetts. But the children playing there in November of 1904 had no thought of legends or ghosts, and it was a complete surprise when part of one wall suddenly collapsed. One of the children was practically buried. The others ran for help, and the owner of the house, William Hyde, and others went to the rescue.

They freed the child and then noticed that there was a hole between the fallen wall and the cellar foundation. In the hole they found a peddler's tin box and close to it the incomplete skeleton of a man. The head was missing.

This evidence settled once and for all a controversy that had raged in the previous century when a family named Fox lived there. They had claimed they experienced weird, ghostly happenings. Their story is one of the most fantastic occult tales of all time.

John Fox, a farmer, lived in the hamlet of Hydesville with his wife and two daughters, Margaretta, 13, and Catherine, 9.

They were a highly respected family, and until they moved into the house in 1848, their life was quiet and unexciting. Then it started. They began to hear inexplicable tapping noises, sometimes soft, sometimes very loud, as if heavy objects were being moved around. Both children became so frightened that their bed had to be moved into their parents' room. Then, the ghostly rappings became so loud and so violent that the beds shook as if an earthquake were rocking them.

The family searched the house, but could find no explanation. The ghostly tapping became progressively louder. Soon the family was completely worn out from lack of sleep.

One night when the noises began, nine-year-old Catherine clapped her hands and challenged the ghost to imitate her. At once her claps were repeated.

Then Mrs. Fox asked the spirit to tap out the ages of her children. To their amazement, the ghost immediately obliged. It even paused for a couple of seconds and then rapped out "three." A third child had died at the age of three.

Joining her daughter, Mrs. Fox asked the spirit to signal with two knocks if it was indeed a spirit, and there followed almost at once two distinct taps. Growing more confident, Mrs. Fox put more questions to the ghost, indicating the number of taps to be given for each specific answer.

In this way, she learned that the spirit was a man who had been murdered when he was 31, and that his body was buried in the cellar of the house. A neighbor, Mr. Duesler, put questions to the ghost, and learned that the killing had been carried out in a bedroom some five years earlier, with a butcher knife, and that not until the night following the murder was the body taken down into the cellar, to be buried 10 feet under the floor of the house.

The spirit also rapped out the information that the killer had been motivated by robbery, stealing $500 from the victim. The cellar was dug up, but nothing was unearthed. This caused many people to accuse the Fox family of manufacturing the whole story.

The following summer, digging was restarted and this time evidence was found—traces of quicklime and charcoal, a plank, hairs, and pieces of bone that a doctor declared had come from a human skull. But no body was found.

Then came more unexpected evidence to support the Fox family's story. Lucretia Pulver, who had been employed as a servant by the former tenants, a Mr. and Mrs. Bell, said that one day a peddler, aged about 30, had called at the house. She had seen him talking with Mrs. Bell, who claimed the man was an old acquaintance.

Lucretia was dismissed by Mrs. Bell that same day, but before she left, she asked the peddler to call at her home before leaving the district, because she wished to buy something from him. He agreed to stop by the next morning, but he never did.

A few days later, she was amazed to be offered her job back by Mrs. Bell. Returning to the house, she saw Mrs. Bell altering some coats, and several things from the peddler's pack were lying around the house.

Sent down to the cellar one evening, Lucretia fell on loose earth. She screamed and Mr. Bell proceeded to fill in what he told her were rat holes.

Lucretia also reported other strange happenings—ghostly rappings and other mysterious sounds. Soon after this, the Bells left the house.

Lucretia's story threw suspicion on Bell, but he was never charged, there being no definite evidence against him.

After the Fox family left, no one went to live in Spook House again.

18. WHAT'S OUT THERE?

A Deadly Game of Cat and Mouse

At 6:30 on the evening of April 1, 1959, a big four-engined C-118 transport aircraft of the USAF's 175th Air Transport Wing roared down the main runway of McChord Air Force Base, near Tacoma, Washington,

and climbed into the southern sky. For the four men on board, this was a routine training mission—so routine that it was virtually automatic.

At 7:45 P.M. the staff in the control tower at McChord Air Force Base heard a frantic distress call from the C-118's pilot. "Mayday! Mayday! We've hit something— or something has hit us! I am returning to base." Then, a few seconds later came a final, desperate scream: "This is it! This is it!" And then there was only silence. The C-118 had crashed into the side of a mountain in the Cascade Range, 30 miles northwest of Mount Rainier's 14,400-foot peak. Air Force crash crews and armed guards raced to the scene. Newsmen and others who attempted to get close were warned off at gunpoint. Explanations and rumors spread like wildfire: had the aircraft been testing some new device? That was unlikely, since the C-118 was only a freighter. Could pilot error be the answer? Or perhaps the C-118 had run into a flock of birds, or collided with another plane? Then— why the secrecy?

But the Air Force knew that none of these reasons was the real one, because a few minutes before the pilot's distress call, the powerful radar at McChord Air Force Base had revealed that the C-118 had picked up three or four mysterious travelling companions— strange, luminous specks of light that darted around the big transport. Gradually, the Air Force specialists who were investigating the crash had built up a minute-by-minute picture of the strange and terrifying fate of the large aircraft.

At seven o'clock on that April evening, residents in the area between Seattle and Mount Rainier had been alarmed by a series of explosions—mysterious detonations that seemed to come from a clear sky. Twenty minutes later, the whole region was shaken by an even bigger bang. About the same time, several bright, luminous objects were seen racing across the sky. They travelled at incredible speed and in complete silence. Many other people witnessed strange flashes and glows around the horizon.

Eyewitnesses in Orting, not far from the scene of the crash, told investigators that the C-118 had appeared overhead at about 7:45 P.M. All the aircraft's four engines had stopped—and a large chunk of its tail was missing. And, strangest of all, the C-118 was being followed by a formation of three shining discs. Every now and then, one of them would break away and dart towards the transport, skipping over it or veering off to one side at the last moment. It was just as though the C-118 were being hounded by a pack of vicious dogs. Several people in the Orting area watched the aircraft and its unearthly companions until they were out of sight.

A minute later, two bright flashes ripped the sky to the northeast. It was at that precise moment that the radio transmission from the C-118 ceased abruptly with the pilot's frantic, "This is it!"

The first rescue teams to arrive at the scene of the crash found a nightmare of charred, twisted metal fragments—hardly any of them more than a foot across—scattered over a whole mountainside. They found three mangled, dislocated bodies, too—sunk deep in the ground by the fearful impact. The fourth body was never found. There was no sign of the plane's tail fin and rudder. They were found much later, miles away in the hills to the north of Mount Rainier.

From the wilderness of torn wreckage, the accident investigators were able to reconstruct exactly how the C-118 had hit the ground, and they came up with a number of facts that baffled them completely. For a start, they calculated that even if the aircraft had nose-dived into the ground under full power, the impact would not have been great enough to rip the machine into such a widely scattered sea of small fragments. But the C-118 had not plowed into the earth nose-first; it had struck on its belly, as though a giant hand had slammed it out of the air with incredible force—just as a person swats a fly.

What happened in those last fateful minutes before the C-118's plunge to earth? Is it beyond the realm of possibility that the aircraft was used as the object of a deadly game of cat and mouse by alien craft—a game that ended in disaster when "they"—whoever or whatever they were—tired of what might have seemed a cumbersome toy and slapped it casually out of the sky?

Killer Sound Waves
from the Sky

One grey February day in 1965, a flock of pigeons winged over the woods near Warminster in England's rural Wiltshire. Suddenly, the winter calm was splintered by a vibrant high-pitched hum that came, as witnesses later testified, "out of the sky."

As though struck by some giant fist, the birds faltered

in mid-air, struggled to regain formation, and then fell, like a shower of stones into the trees below. Every pigeon was dead, killed apparently instantaneously by mysterious waves of sound.

There was a government investigation, but no scientific theorizing could explain away the attacks on both animals and humans from something violent and invisible in the sky. The file is still open.

It began in the early hours of Christmas Day, 1964, when people were jerked abruptly from their sleep by strange, frightening noises above the rooftops.

A witness said later: "There were crashes, thuds and clatters, as though someone was bombarding the houses with gigantic rocks—and in the background was a high-pitched hum, vibrating on the frosty air."

But outside in the darkness, nothing could be seen, although stone walls shook with echoing vibrations.

Then suddenly, the noises stopped. Puzzled and alarmed, the people of Warminster went back to bed. Some blamed the army: there was a military camp near Warminster. But the army didn't usually carry out exercises on Christmas morning, and the mysterious sounds did not remotely resemble explosions.

The sonic bombardments lasted for six hours on that memorable Christmas morning. No one could come up with a reasonable explanation. But the noises seemed to

276

have died away—for good, it was hoped.

Then, in February, 1965, the sounds from the sky began again, with another strange mid-air massacre of pigeons. And this time the attacks began to take a vicious turn.

One person who felt their full fury was a 19-year-old farmer who was walking along a dark, deserted road after seeing his girlfriend home. The night was silent, all sound blanketed by dense fog.

At first, the youth didn't take much notice of a faint humming noise. Then it swelled into a shrill, ear-splitting screech, "as though all the devils in hell had been let loose."

All at once, a fearsome, bone-crushing pressure clamped down on the young man, forcing him to his knees in the road. An icy, stinging wind tore at his face, and noiseless waves of inexplicable pressure buffeted his body. His head felt as though it were held in iron clamps. Then the pressure lifted, as suddenly as it had descended, and he staggered home. His parents took one look at his white, terrified face and sent for the doctor, who treated the young man for severe shock.

Animals suffered most severely from the assaults. After one weird burst of ultra-sound, dozens of field mice were found lying dead in a field. Their fur was singed and their bodies perforated with tiny holes. Dogs and cats became ill, and canaries and budgerigars toppled dead from their perches.

The violent sound attacks lasted—on and off—until the end of June, 1965. Scientists and government investigators arrived at Warminster and the surrounding area to study the phenomenon and came away baffled.

Is there any rational explanation? Were the sound waves that battered Warminster a product of natural causes—or something else?

And can it be pure coincidence that the place in Britain where the greatest number of corroborated UFO sightings have occurred is Warminster?

Did Michael Norton Fall Through a Hole in Time?

One of the most uncanny stories I have ever come across concerns the baffling disappearance of a Canadian farmer's son, 12-year-old Michael Norton, on a November morning over 60 years ago. The hunt for the missing child went on for years, because although he disappeared physically, both his parents and hundreds of investigators all heard Michael's voice—calling faintly from the same few square feet of ground.

On the day it happened, Michael overslept. When he rushed down to breakfast, he was seen by his father and mother, an aunt, and two farm workers. A few minutes later his mother watched him trudge towards the cow shed. She had no way of knowing that neither she nor anybody else would ever see the boy again.

Some hours later, wondering about his absence, Ruth Norton called Michael to come back to the house or he would be late for school. Michael's younger brother and sister were impatiently waiting for him to take them into the village.

There was no answer to Mrs. Norton's call and, with some irritation, her husband put on his boots and went out to fetch the boy. When he entered the barn, it was empty. The stool and bucket were there, the latter half full of milk. Michael had obviously stopped in the middle of his work—but there was no sign of him.

Mr. Norton searched the barn. He found nothing. He called his family and the workmen and they combed the farm and its environs. There was no trace of the boy.

Seriously alarmed, Mr. Norton drove into the nearby township of Burtons Falls and alerted the police. A few hours later, the police arrived at the farm with a bloodhound, which was given Michael's scent. The animal's keen nose soon detected Michael's trail. It led from the kitchen door into the barn and then out of the barn again, straight into the open south pasture, a field visible from both the house and the nearby road.

Then the bloodhound, which had been tugging excitedly at the leash, suddenly stopped in its tracks. They were in the middle of the pasture, several dozen yards from the farther boundary. Surprised, the handler urged the dog on, but the animal just whined. The trail had disappeared!

What happened? No one ever found out. Search parties were organized and other tracker dogs brought, but none of them ever uncovered a hint of the boy's movements after he had stood in the middle of the field. Michael Norton had literally disappeared into thin air!

A few nights later, when hope of finding their son alive was fading, the Nortons were overjoyed to hear a voice outside. It was Michael's, and it called one word that no other boy would call in that place: "Mum!"

They rushed outside, shouting with relief, and then stopped. There was no one there! The voice called again, "Mum!" It was Michael, both were certain of that. But they searched and searched and found nothing. They called his name and he didn't answer. Half an hour later, as they stood in the farmyard, peering hopelessly into the dark, they heard him again: "Mum," and this time he clearly added, "Where are you?"

Many people came to the little farm, and many of them heard the lost voice as it called and pleaded for help. One of the most logical theories that was put forth suggested that he had tumbled into an underground river, an old well, or simply a crack in the ground. But this idea was eventually discarded when experts studied the terrain. A primitive form of aerial photography was also used, hoping to pinpoint a fault in the field. But there was no evidence to suggest such a thing.

For weeks, the frantic parents and others heard the disembodied voice of Michael Norton, which was growing fainter as the days passed. It seemed that he was in a thick mist, but quite free to move. Then, after a while, he was heard no more.

Is it possible that some unknown physical law opened a "gap" in time, through which Michael fell or was pulled? And that such a suspension of the normal laws would be visible to the human eye, maybe as a "mist," or some other alteration of the light?

Might it be this disturbance that Michael saw? Might he have run across the field to see for himself, and been swallowed up in the middle of the pasture, which was, for a brief moment, the "eye" in the needle of time?

Death Watch

From the time John Phillips entered the hospital in September, 1952, until his death a few months later, the hospital staff at St. Olive's, in the town of Biddeford in Devon, England, became increasingly alarmed by strange events surrounding the patient. Phillips was an old man in his late 70s, terribly confused and incapable of carrying on a sensible conversation.

Often, under the ward's dim, orange night lights, the atmosphere would appear to be alive and full of movement around John's bed—like heat waves, wavering and fluctuating. But it was the soft persistent *voices* that sent the night nurses rushing out of the ward in terror. Each time anyone investigated to find out who was talking to Phillips, the old man was always fast asleep. And when any of the staff crept up to the bed to listen to the voices, which were always indistinguishable, the noise would stop—abruptly.

A student nurse received a severe reprimand from the night nurse when she reported that she had heard a large animal padding around the ward, but when the older nurse approached the ward, she too heard the clicking of claws on the hard, polished floor.

When she called for help, two doctors and a night porter rushed into the ward to catch the animal, but a thorough search revealed nothing.

Over the next few weeks, nurses often turned up the main lights, crawled about on all fours, and peered under the rows of beds in an attempt to track down the animal. Often the swift, stealthy padding appeared to brush past them. And then they would hear heavy breathing and smell a strong animal odor.

Patients frequently heard the creature also, and many asked that Phillips be removed to a private room. But because of a shortage of beds, this was not possible. The hospital board finally dismissed the footsteps as being either rats running under the flooring, creaking timbers—or just plain imagination.

On a Wednesday morning, 12 days after Phillips had

been put in the ward, there came a manifestation that could not be rejected so easily.

Two young nurses were startled to see a head peeping out from behind the heavy, lined curtains drawn across the window at the head of Phillips' bed. The features were those of a young man with dark, curly hair, and they had never seen him before!

Since visitors were not allowed in the wards at six in the morning, the nurses hurried to the window, and as they did, the head withdrew and the curtains fell together again.

The curtains were still moving as one of the nurses pushed them open, but nothing was there—except the closed window, securely locked from the inside.

The screams of the second nurse brought the medical staff to the ward from all parts of the hospital, and again a thorough search was made without anything being discovered.

It was a closely locked ward. The outside windowsills were about nine feet from the ground, and beyond that was a 12-foot wall topped with iron spikes and a thick ledge of glass splinters.

How could any intruder withdraw his head and shoulders and disappear within seconds, closing and locking the window from the opposite side?

Later the same day, after an emergency meeting,

Phillips was removed to a private room. Two experienced nurses were assigned to him. Shortly after one in the morning, both nurses heard voices from within the private room, but every time they checked, Phillips was sound asleep and no one else was present.

Two hours later, they distinctly heard a loud chuckle, and to their horror saw a face protruding from between the curtains of the only window in the room.

The description given by the nurses was the same as that of the person who had been seen before. As they stood rooted to the spot, the face laughed and then vanished.

The window, again, was securely locked. One of the nurses noticed that the temperature of the room had dropped considerably, although the radiators were so hot that it was impossible to touch them with bare hands.

Less than three hours later, John Phillips died. Never again did anyone in the hospital report hearing the strange murmuring voices, or the animal sounds, or seeing any mysterious visitors.

19. HORROR
BEYOND
REASON

The Dark Evil That Haunts Walsingham House

It was difficult to say just when the Walsingham family realized that there was something different about the house—something evil. Certainly, it was before they went in and opened the shuttered windows.

They hadn't been away that long. It was only 10 days since Howard Walsingham had left the house with his wife, their teenage son and daughters, and cat and dog— to visit with relatives and attend a wedding in Charleston, South Carolina, over 100 miles away.

Their farmhouse, which lay on the outskirts of the small town of Oakville, had always been a happy one. But on this spring day in 1889, everyone felt that something was wrong.

The dog, Don Caesar, refused to enter the place. When young Howard dragged him in, he broke into furious snarling and barking. His back bristled with rage. This happened several times. As the day went on, he continued to act strangely, as if terrified.

Later, after a neighbor and his wife came to welcome them home, Walsingham heard whines and growls from one of the rooms. When he went to investigate, he saw that Don Caesar seemed to have gone mad. The big hound leaped into the air as if going for a man's throat, but suddenly he fell back, as if he had received a heavy blow, and lay motionless on the floor.

When Walsingham picked up the dog, its neck had been broken. It was dead.

That evening, around dusk, the house was suddenly filled with shouts and hideous laughter. This was heard by everybody, including the neighbors, and it put them all in a state of near-panic.

Then Amelia, the older daughter, brushing her hair in front of a mirror, plainly saw a man's hand resting on her shoulder. But there was no reflection of it in the mirror, nor any sign of an arm or body.

Walsingham, in the garden, saw footprints forming on the dust of the path in front of him as he walked. Yet nothing mortal could be seen.

As uncanny and terrifying as these events were, they paled into insignificance before the incident that took place later that evening.

The family and neighbors were sitting at supper when loud, terrible groans started coming from the room above. The sounds stopped, and talk began again, until someone remarked on a stain of what looked like blood on the white tablecloth. Young Howard then pointed to the ceiling. A liquid was slowly dripping down onto the table from a patch of red. It was so like fresh blood that they couldn't finish the meal. Instead, they watched, horrified, as the liquid continued to drip. It occurred to them all that some terrible deed, some ghastly murder, was taking place upstairs.

Walsingham raced upstairs, followed by his son, and flung open the door, dreading what he might see. But the room was empty.

Pulling up the carpet, they found the floorboards soaked with the same red, gruesome liquid that was dripping into the room below. But there was no explanation.

After an uncomfortable night, Walsingham rode into Oakville and gave a sample of the liquid to the local doctor, who examined it under a microscope. It was unquestionably, he said, human blood.

These incidents were too much for the Walsinghams, who soon moved to another side of town.

Questioned about anything unusual that might have taken place before the macabre events, Walsingham did remember one incident. The day before the family left for the wedding, a farmhand asked Walsingham to look at a pile of old dried bones that had been turned up by the plow. Not able to decide whether or not they were human, Walsingham ordered them thrown into a limekiln.

A spiritualist group suggested that the spirit of the man whose bones were treated to such an indignity might have summoned dark forces to his aid to make the place uninhabitable by mortals. It seems unlikely that a pile of dried bones could produce such terrifying phenomena. But, as yet, no one has come up with a better explanation.

Room of Sighs

It seemed such a peaceful, comfortable old place, the house in County Down, in Northern Ireland—and so it was. Except in one of the upstairs bedrooms.

My grandfather, Cecil Macklin, rented the house in July of 1912. A few days after moving in, he was shaving at the mirror in his bedroom when he heard it for the first time.

From somewhere within that room, from a few feet behind him, he heard a loud, shuddering sigh. Yet, when he glanced around, there was nobody there.

At first, he thought he had imagined the whole business. Then he heard it again. But he chose to ignore it. He had an idea that his children were playing a joke on him.

So when he left his room, he crept silently along the passage to his children's bedroom and whipped the door open. To his amazement, the children were all fast asleep.

Of course, he didn't mention the incident to anyone, since he still wasn't sure he had heard anything. But within the next few days he heard the sighing again. It always happened during the evening.

Soon, he noticed that the servants in the house came up with all sorts of excuses rather than enter the room, but when he questioned them, all they could tell him was that something there frightened them.

After that, he decided to investigate the phenomenon for himself. He went up to the room in the afternoon and sat in the rocking chair reading. As evening crept down from the mountainside, he became aware of a coldness that filled the room.

Determined to wait for the sighing to begin, he stayed in the chair until it was too dark to read. Then he heard it again. And it almost terrified him out of his wits. For the moaning and sighing seemed to boom out right in his ear, and he realized that it was coming from the chair in which he was sitting!

Springing up, he stared at the chair that was now rocking wildly. Then, all at once, something even more weird happened. The chair stopped rocking—almost as if some invisible hand had halted it!

The heavy sighing was still behind him, and as he moved across the room to light the lamp, it followed him. Suddenly, all his courage deserted him and he rushed for the door—the moaning and breathing pursuing him all the way, until he had wrenched the door open and slammed it behind him.

But as he leaned against it and turned the key in the lock, he could quite clearly hear *something* snuffling and grunting on the other side of the door.

For the rest of the summer the room was kept locked and none of the family ever went in there again.

But the haunting didn't stop at that.

Some weeks later, when weekend guests were staying at the house, two of the men walking outside saw a strange, pinkish glow coming from the window of that room.

They dashed into the house, shouting "Fire!" and rushed up the stairs. The room was locked, but a strange smell was coming through and they could see a bright light beneath the door.

It was a stout, heavy door, and they couldn't smash it down, so one of the men hurried down the stairs to get an ax. Just as he returned to the top of the stairs, the door flew open. The other man cowered back in horror as a pink light blazed forward. Then a shadow blotted it out and two strong, muscular arms came from the room, pulled him inside, and slammed the door shut.

There was a scream, and the second man began crashing the ax down on the door panels. My grandfather joined him and they forced the door open. They found the room in darkness—and their friend lying unconscious on the floor. They carried him out—and behind them, something sighed—a heavy, despairing sigh, that neither wanted to investigate further!

When their friend came to, he couldn't say what had happened to him. All that he remembered was the door springing open and a dazzling bright light blinding him for a few moments before somebody pulled him into *a dark room*. Then he fainted.

In the morning, everybody left that house—forever, as it turned out—and spent the rest of the weekend in a nearby inn.

None of the local people were surprised by their vacating the house. What was surprising was that it had only been a few months earlier that the house had first achieved the reputation of being haunted. Before then, it had been occupied by the same family for over 200 years, and during that time it had been a happy home.

Then, early in 1912, after it had been sold, it was being renovated. One of the workmen was alone in that bedroom, plastering part of the wall. Suddenly he heard a sigh.

At first, he thought it had been caused by a draft, or the wind outside. Then he realized that it was coming from within that very room—from a few yards away— but there was nobody there. Nothing, except the shadows dancing in the flickering light from his lamp.

But what made the flame flicker? There was nothing to explain it.

Then the rocking chair, which had been absolutely motionless until that moment, started to sway gently back and forth, exactly as if somebody were sitting in it.

From then on, the workmen refused to go into the room except by twos, and then only in daylight.

The house is still there, and it's still occupied, but the people living there don't use the room except to store their unwanted bits and pieces. And the door is still kept locked.

Killer Tree of the Cameroons

All that was left of the campfire was a smoldering glow deep in the wood ash, but Bob Fellows, huddled snugly in his sleeping bag beneath the old tree, didn't notice that, in the last few moments before the African dawn.

Something had roused him from his sleep, and for a moment he lay there wondering what was wrong. Then he heard a rustling noise from the tree above his head, and a few moments later, a weird, gurgling moan. Thinking that there might be a leopard or some other animal about to attack, he snatched up his flashlight and rifle and turned to waken his partner, Mike Cura.

That was when he saw it. Mike Cura's sleeping bag had been ripped to shreds and there wasn't a sign of him. Then something whipped through the darkness and smashed against Fellows' shoulder.

The blow sent him spinning across the ground and half stunned him, but a choked scream brought him to his senses. The cry came from up among the branches of the tree, and training his flashlight on them, Fellows saw a horrifying sight.

His partner's body was being slowly and powerfully crushed to death by the branches of the tree. One branch had wrapped itself around his throat and was strangling him, while several other, thicker ones were exerting such pressure on his body that Fellows could almost hear the bones splintering.

Then, slowly, when the life had been squeezed out of the victim, the grotesque killer tree unraveled its branches and let Cura's body fall limply to the ground.

Fellows remained where he was, too horrified and too

frightened to move, as the uncannily arm-like branches groped blindly towards him. But they couldn't quite reach him.

Fellows stood there until the first streaks of daylight. The tree gave a heavy, shuddering sigh, and its branches seemed to lose their life.

Four days later, in May 1903, Fellows was telling police in Iloku, in the Cameroons, that his partner had been murdered by a tree! Of course, the authorities didn't believe his story. Fellows was held on suspicion of murder, while an expedition set out to recover Cura's body.

When the body was brought back to Iloku, an inquest was held, but the results of it were so startling that they were not made public for many years. Fellows was, however, freed from jail and the charge was quietly dismissed. For the doctors who carried out the postmortem stated that Fellows *could not* have killed his friend; the damage had been inflicted by some powerful, *superhuman* creature. One doctor said that he doubted if even a gorilla would have possessed the strength to mutilate a body so severely.

Shortly afterwards, a missionary working in that district heard about Cura's death and wrote Iloku authorities about similar incidents.

Apparently, 12 men had been found dead at the base

of that tree within a period of 50 years, and for centuries the African tribesmen had treated that particular stretch of forest as *taboo*.

The origins of the legend were based on a tribal priest about 80 years earlier, a man named Ubo, who suddenly went berserk and started a campaign of terror in the region. Many people were waylaid by him and strangled to death for no reason at all.

At last the warriors set out to hunt the killer down. They trapped Ubo beneath the tree one evening during a thunderstorm. As they closed in for the kill, there was a flash of lightning. The tree was struck, and so was Ubo, who had been standing with his back to the trunk. When the tribesmen recovered his body, they found that both his hands had been sliced off at the wrists by the lightning. Yet the warriors couldn't find the missing hands anywhere.

It was soon after that, according to the missionary, that the tree started to gain the reputation of being a "strangler" tree.

But that wasn't the end of the story.

Less than six months after the death of Mike Cura, a boy from the mission school staggered into Iloku to gasp out an incredible story to the police. The missionary had been killed by the tree—right before the boy's own eyes.

The boy had gone with the missionary to chop down

the tree and destroy it once and for all. But they hadn't arrived there until late evening, and while the boy started a camp, the missionary approached the tree with an ax.

Even before the blade hit into the tree trunk, the boy heard the missionary scream in terror. He turned just in time to see thick branches wrapping themselves around the man's body.

The police inspector who went to investigate found the dead missionary hanging limply in a fork in the tree trunk. By then it was morning and the tree seemed nothing more than just a dead tree.

However, the inspector and his patrol had instructions to destroy it—which they did. With a loud groan, the mighty trunk crashed to the ground. Then it was chopped and sawed into logs that were piled in a heap to be burned.

Before this could happen, a strange and gruesome discovery was made. As one of the soldiers split a log, he found two human, skeleton hands trapped within the wood. Both hands had been severed at the wrists.

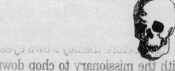

20. UNCANNY!

Steer to the Nor' West...

The Hunter and the Hunted

The ghost of an elephant control officer is often seen roaming in the bush in Zimbabwe, some 20 miles from Serenje. It's as if he is still doing his duty: hunting down rogue elephants and keeping them away from the farm country.

Although it was sometimes Richard James's job to kill the great beasts, he made no secret of the fact that he had an enormous respect—even affection—for the elephants.

He frequently spoke of them as the gentlemen of the jungle, wise, courteous and affectionate, and said that when he had to die, he only hoped that he would be killed by an elephant. He got his wish.

On one of his tours from his base at Serenje, he penetrated deep into the bush, chasing a rogue elephant. When he caught up with it, he hit the elephant with his first shot, but failed to kill it. Then, when the wounded and infuriated animal charged him, his gun misfired.

Everything happened so quickly that his bearers were unable to shoot before the animal reached him and hurled him into a tree.

After the elephant was killed, they climbed the tree and gently brought James back to the ground. They carried him a short way, but his back was broken and he knew he was dying. His final request was to be buried at the spot where he had fallen. He wanted to stay in the bush country forever.

His bearers soon prepared a grave, and after a short burial ceremony made the long trek back to Serenje, where they reported the tragic accident.

The story should have ended there. But when the news of James's death eventually reached officialdom, whoever received it failed to understand the significance of the dead man's request. A month later, a special expedition was sent to exhume his body and take it back to the European cemetery at Mpika, near Serenje.

But when the expedition arrived, the grave was surrounded by elephants. Each time someone moved in the direction of the grave, the elephants became angry and charged.

Two days passed; a number of elephants were killed, and eventually the body was recovered and the expedition went back to Mpika.

John Littler was appointed to be James's replacement, and six weeks after the funeral he heard that elephants in that area were causing a great deal of disturbance and damage. He decided to go back to the place where the accident had occurred, but had great difficulty persuading his bearers to go with him. It was as if they had a premonition of what was about to happen.

The party was within 100 yards of the original grave when one of the bearers gave a terrible scream, dropped the supplies he was carrying, and ran back along the path.

He was quickly followed by all the native bearers. Littler and his assistant stood alone, surrounded by supplies that lay where the bearers had dropped them as they fled.

Then both men saw the cause of the panic. For there, standing near the grave, surrounded by a large herd of elephants, was Richard James.

Littler knew that it could not be James. He had helped to bury his colleague. It had to be his ghost.

Both men moved forward, and as they did, several elephants lifted their trunks, bellowed, and turned as if to prevent them from reaching the grave.

The ghost seemed to wave them back. It was as if he was warning the two men that if they came any nearer they could easily be killed by the elephants, who by now were very angry indeed.

Littler decided to heed the warning, and the two men retreated, leaving the ghost of Richard James with his beloved elephants. Since 1958, many officials and hunters have reported seeing the ghost within a mile of the spot where he was killed.

Was this a classic case of a man "returning" because of a guilty conscience? Or did he possess a curiously involved relationship with his enemy—the strong affinity that so often exists between the hunter and the hunted?

The Riddle of the Seabird

The crowd waited patiently as the sailing ship *Seabird* made her way towards shore. They didn't know it, but they were witnessing one of the greatest sea mysteries of all time.

The *Seabird* was completing a voyage from Honduras to Easton's Beach, near Newport, Rhode Island.

But suddenly, instead of heading for the landing place, the *Seabird* swung off course. Picking up speed, it sailed swiftly towards the long, dangerous reef that lay a mile out. Its sails were full as the ship gathered speed. The crowd gasped, for many boats had met their end on the killer strip of jagged rock.

The skipper must have gone mad, everybody thought in amazement, as they waited for the inevitable catastrophe.

But there was no crash, no crunching of timber. Just as the crowd prepared themselves for horror on that Sunday morning in November, 1850, they witnessed a miracle. At the very last second, a great swell lifted the ship and swept her clear over the reef. The *Seabird* kept going as if nothing had happened—until she came to rest a few yards from the beach.

For several moments the crowd stood in silence. Then, recovering from their amazement and terror, they cheered. But only echoes answered them. Not a sound came from the ship now floating peacefully in the shallow water.

When no one appeared on deck, some of the bystanders waded out to investigate. When they boarded the *Seabird,* they found only one sign of human life—the captain's dog, a well-fed and affectionate mongrel. The skipper and his crew of more than 30 men had vanished without a trace—and probably only minutes earlier—while the ship was in sight of shore!

A pot of coffee was simmering gently on the stove, and it had not been made long. All the instruments were working perfectly. The skipper had noted in his log book that the ship had passed Branton Reef—just two miles offshore from Newport—within sight of the watchers on shore.

Puzzled and alarmed, the locals called in the police, who found nothing. A blank was also drawn by experts who went over the ship from stem to stern.

A sea search was organized in the hope that some of the missing crew might be picked up. But none were. At last, orders were given for the ship to be unloaded. As the cargo was taken ashore, careful watch was kept for any clue to what had happened to the crew in the two miles between Branton Reef and the shore. It took four days to unload the *Seabird*—and no ship had ever been emptied more carefully. But still there was no trace of the crew.

Baffled, the police gave up and the experts returned to their various headquarters. A message was sent to the owners of the *Seabird* to send a new crew to take her back to sea.

They never did, for early one morning, exactly one week after she arrived, the *Seabird* vanished, slipping out to sea as mysteriously as she had arrived. Like her crew, the *Seabird* was never seen again.

The Man Who Projected Himself

One of the weirdest and most baffling types of psychic phenomena is the inexplicable power of certain people to project themselves from one place to another. While they remain physically in one place, they may be seen many miles away—appearing, at least, to be quite real.

Perhaps the most extraordinary case was related at sea in the year 1860 by Captain John Clarke, master of the schooner *Julia Hallock*, trading between Cuba and New York. He had heard it from a seaman named Robert Bruce from Devon, England.

Bruce, according to Clarke, was an honest and upright man who would not have lied about anything. He was also a first-class seaman, having risen to first mate by the time he was 30.

Bruce had been serving on a vessel plying from Liverpool, England, to New Brunswick, in eastern Canada. His strange experiences took place after six weeks at sea. Darkness had fallen and Bruce went to the captain's cabin to work out some navigational calculations.

Bruce, intent upon his figures, did not notice that the captain stepped out of the cabin. When he had arrived at a conclusion, he announced their present longitude and latitude without looking up.

Receiving no reply, he raised his head and was astonished to see that not only had the captain gone, but that a complete stranger was sitting at the writing table.

Bruce was a man of more than average courage, but the sight of the strange man's keen eyes boring into his filled him with sudden apprehension. He did not stop to ask questions but fled and sought out the captain, who was back on the bridge.

Seeing Bruce's white face, the captain commented, "You look as if you've seen a ghost."

Bruce said: "Who is that man sitting at your desk, sir—in your cabin?"

The captain stared. "There is no man in my cabin—and if you saw anyone you must be seeing things, Mr. Bruce."

When Bruce insisted that he had seen a strange man, the captain suggested that it must have been another crew member.

"It was not, sir—I know every man in the clew well enough to know that this man was a complete stranger to me," Bruce insisted.

The captain, realizing his mate was in earnest, ordered Bruce to go back to his cabin and ask the stranger to step up to the bridge. But Bruce was afraid now, without knowing precisely why. He said he would rather not go back to the cabin alone.

At first the captain was angry and ordered Bruce not to be ridiculous. Finally he went down to the cabin with Bruce. It was empty. But then they both saw some writing on the captain's slate. The words were: *Steer to the Nor'West*.

The captain called to the cabin every man who might have entered it on some duty or other, and made each in turn write out the same words. None matched the writing on the slate.

"Do you believe in ghosts, Mr. Bruce?" the captain asked.

Bruce said he did not.

"Nor do I believe in such things," said the captain. "But all the same, I think we will sail that way—just to see what does happen."

In the middle of the next afternoon, the lookout reported sighting an iceberg. When the captain and Bruce trained their glasses on it, they saw a vessel trapped in the ice.

The ship was a schooner on her way from Quebec to Liverpool with about 60 passengers. Water and food were dangerously low. The crew and passengers were in a sorry plight. Had Bruce's ship not sailed that way, all might have died of starvation and exposure.

Bruce was on deck supervising the rescue operation when one man in a very weak condition was hoisted aboard. Bruce went to assist him, and when the passenger lifted his head, Bruce recognized the face.

It was the very same man he had seen sitting in the captain's cabin—miles from that spot!

When he was feeling stronger, the passenger was asked to go to the cabin and write on the slate the words *Steer to the Nor'West.* He did so, and the writing was found to be exactly the same!

The passenger obviously could not have written the message, trapped as he was on the ice-bound ship. And when asked, he said that he did not recall even having a dream in which he wrote such a message.

But the captain of the wrecked vessel reported that at the hour when Bruce saw the stranger in the cabin, the man had been in a very deep sleep. When he awoke, he had said something strange: "Captain, we shall be rescued very soon now—by sunset tomorrow at the very latest."

And the passenger went on to tell the captain that he had dreamed of being aboard a strange ship that was coming to the rescue. He even described the ship in detail as he came out of his deep, trance-like sleep—although he did not remember the dream ten minutes later.

The description, which the captain remembered distinctly, fitted Bruce's ship exactly.

dream in which he wrote such a message.

21. ENCOUNTERS WITH GHOSTS

Portrait of a Ghost

It was the summer of 1913, and Lebrun, a promising young artist, had only been in Paris for a few weeks. A shy man, especially in the company of women, it took some courage for him to speak to the young girl he saw standing beneath the street lamp in Montmartre. She was looking about her so helplessly—so obviously uncertain of her whereabouts—that Lebrun finally decided to go to her assistance.

She turned towards him—and his first reaction was astonishment, because he had never seen a more beautiful face! And instead of offering to assist her, he found himself begging her to pose for him.

For several moments she stared at him with a puzzled, frightened expression in her eyes. Then, slowly, she replied:

"A portrait would take several sittings and my time here is very short. Tonight I am with you—but tomorrow I have no idea where—"

Lebrun resolved to finish the painting in one night, and he pleaded so hard that she finally nodded and walked along silently beside him.

When they reached his studio, he set to work at once. She was a perfect study in black and white; her face had a pale, almost deathly hue about it and her clothes were coarse and black. She had a black band high on her throat, and when Lebrun asked her to remove it, she stared at him in terror—and shook her head.

As Lebrun worked through the early hours of that morning, the girl sat perfectly still, perfectly silent.

The first cold light of the new day was over the horizon when Lebrun finished painting. It was a perfect likeness, except for the black band, which he had decided not to incorporate into the picture.

The girl left without even saying goodbye. Lebrun

hurried after her, but she had disappeared into the early-morning gloom. And apart from the sound of her footsteps dying away in the distance, it was almost as if she had never existed.

Later that day his landlady came to the studio to collect Lebrun's rent. She took one look at the portrait on the easel and exclaimed, "What a good likeness of Gretel Pederson! You must have seen her photograph in the papers after she was guillotined for murdering her parents and her husband."

Lebrun stared at her. He hadn't heard about the murder and surely had not seen the girl's photograph.

After pacing his room for hours, he decided that he must have been overworking. The whole thing must have been a figment of his imagination—he must have glanced at her photograph in the papers and somehow it had registered in his subconscious.

Just as he was deciding to take things easier, he heard a knocking at his door. It was Julien Sant, an artist friend.

"Lebrun, you can call me a madman if you like—but last night I saw a ghost!"

Sant went on: "It was early evening, about eight o'clock, in the streets near here. There was a young girl and I was obsessed by the thought that I had seen her somewhere before. I just saw her as I passed, but I could never forget that beautiful face.

"Today I went along to the newspaper files, and I saw her photograph. It was Gretel Pederson!"

Lebrun said nothing. Instead he pointed to the picture.

"That's her, all right," said Sant. "But when I saw her she had a high black band around her throat."

Sant added, "And that's not all. I found out that last night was the anniversary of her *death.* . . !"

The Corpse That Walked Away to Die Again

The fiercest blizzard Scotland had known for over 50 years had been raging for almost four days in February, 1963, when Joe Turnbull's truck ran into a snow drift high on the remote Beattock Summit in Lanarkshire. There were hundreds of other vehicles abandoned along the road.

Turnbull realized that if he stayed where he was, it might be days before he was reported missing, and by then, it would be too late. So he set out to walk to the nearest village.

The whirling snow, hurled at him by a biting cold wind, made it impossible to see more than a few feet in front of him. That was why he didn't see the body lying facedown in the center of the road until he stumbled over it.

Slowly, Turnbull freed the body of a bearded young man from the freezing snow and wrapped his red, brightly patterned scarf around the head to protect it from the cold. The man appeared to be dead.

Turnbull wasn't sure about that, though, and he couldn't walk away and leave the man lying there, because if he weren't dead, he soon would be.

Lifting the unconscious man onto his shoulders, Joe started trudging through three-foot-deep snow drifts to Beattock village. It was almost two miles away, but now two lives depended upon his succeeding.

Some time later, when he was almost fainting from exhaustion, he heard voices and saw the gleam of flashlights. To his relief, two men came striding through the snow. When they saw him almost on his knees with the body across his shoulders, they hurried to assist him.

The darkness, the thickly falling snow, and their hooded jackets hid their faces, but as they took the unconscious—or dead—man from Turnbull, they exchanged details.

They, too, were truck drivers, they said. And when

Turnbull explained about the body, they offered to take it with them to a railway station a few miles across the fields. Turnbull was invited to accompany them, but since he could see the lights of the village, he decided to press on.

Then the two strangers, carrying the limp body between them, disappeared into the storm. And disappeared is the only word to describe what followed. For neither the truck drivers nor the "corpse" were ever seen again.

Joe Turnbull reported the incident to the police, but when they checked with the trucking companies the two strangers were supposed to work for, they found no record of any people with those names ever having been employed. As the storm slackened off, police launched a search for the two men and their burden.

There was always the danger that they had all perished in the blizzard, but no bodies answering their descriptions were discovered. And no men had reached the railway station either that night or in the 48 hours afterwards.

Then there was the scarf that Turnbull had wrapped around the "corpse's" head. It had still been there when the other men carried him off, but during the intensive police hunt all over the moors, the scarf was never recovered.

But it *was seen* again! A motorist who had abandoned

his vehicle a few hours later that night, several miles on the other side of Beattock village, later told police how he and his wife had met a young man answering that description. He had been bearded and was wearing a *brightly patterned red scarf around his head*!

The three of them had walked together towards the village, but somehow during the height of the blizzard, the young man had fallen behind. And although they called out to him and hunted back along the road for a few hundred yards, they failed to find him again.

Soon afterwards people started reporting a ghost on Beattock Summit—the ghost of a young, bearded man wearing a colorful scarf around his head. The man stands at the roadside trying to thumb a lift from passing cars. Whenever a car pulls up, the young man vanishes.

Herne the Hunter

Arnold Beckett's favorite place was Windsor Great Park. There was nothing he liked doing better than strolling for hours through the magnificent forest. Soon, he came to know practically every inch of the area.

One autumn twilight in 1931, when Beckett was about to make his way back to the station to catch a train home to London, he realized that there was something different about the park. There was something different especially about the clearing he had walked through a few moments earlier. For in the center of it was a huge tree—and he was sure that he had never seen one there before.

Beckett stopped and stared at the tree for a long time, wondering if he had perhaps confused this clearing with some other. But he was so convinced that there had been *no* tree there that he began to feel quite nervous.

Then, as he walked around the tree, he saw something horrible and grotesque. Hanging from a lower limb, a corpse was swaying on the end of a rope!

His first instinct was to cut the man down, but as he hurried forward to do this, his feet sank into the long grass and he stumbled on a loose branch. To keep from falling on his face, he threw his hands forward to break his fall.

His eyes couldn't have left the tree for more than a split second, and yet, when he looked again, there was nothing there. No hanging man and no tree.

Beckett's heart raced with fear. He had no idea what was happening, but he knew that he wanted to get away from that place as fast as he could!

For a time he kept his strange experience to himself. But later he did tell what had happened, and then he learned from a schoolmaster in Windsor that what he had most likely seen in the forest had been the ghost of Herne the Hunter.

Herne the Hunter had been a forest warden when Henry VIII was on the throne—but more than that, he was said to have practiced witchcraft under a certain tree in the park. And it was from that tree that Herne had hanged himself. For centuries his specter had been known to haunt the forest and it had been seen many times before.

His appearance, however, was a certain omen of disaster.

Beckett was fascinated by the legend, but he remained skeptical about the appearance of the ghostly tree being an omen of disaster.

Then six months later, after Beckett's business unexpectedly failed, he committed suicide. He hanged himself from a tree in Windsor Great Park.

22. SKIRMISHES WITH THE SUPERNATURAL

The Sacred Cat

His fatal encounter with the mummy case was not the first terrifying situation that archaeologist Gordon Richardson had faced with an object from one of the Egyptian tombs. There had been his spine-chilling experience with the sacred cat.

The mummy of the cat was contained in a small coffin

when native workmen brought it out of the tomb of one of the Pharaohs. Why they then put the unopened mummy case in Richardson's hotel room remains a mystery. They didn't tell him about it. And when he returned to his room after dark, he stumbled over the small coffin and nearly broke his neck.

The coffin was made in the shape of a sitting cat and was in two shell-like sections. Inside would be a mummified cat sitting upright, embalmed and wrapped in cloth.

Richardson left the case where it was. When he went to bed it was still sitting there in the center of the room, staring at him with its painted eyes.

In the middle of the night, he was awakened by a noise like a pistol shot. As he sprang up, a large grey cat sprang across his bed, clawed his hand viciously, and dashed away through the open window.

By the time Richardson recovered from his shock, he was startled to see by the light of the moon that the two sides of the coffin had burst apart and were still rocking to a standstill on the floor. Between them sat the sacred embalmed cat, swathed in bandages.

When he scrambled out of bed, a chill swept over him. The bandages on the mummified cat had been savagely torn open at the throat—as if by an animal clawing its way to freedom.

Richardson knew that ancient Egyptians believed

that the souls of the dead left the body by way of the throat. But another idea was forming in his mind—one that belied a lifetime of rational thinking and all his scientific training. He could not help toying with the seemingly preposterous idea that the sacred cat had torn itself free from its bonds—and that the grey cat that attacked him was the mummified cat's escaping spirit.

Of course, Richardson said later, there was a perfectly straightforward explanation for the entire experience. It was possible that the brittle wooden coffin had broken open because of the accidental kick he had given it—and perhaps because of the change of atmosphere from the dry desert to the more humid banks of the Nile.

And the grey cat probably had wandered into his bedroom from the village, possibly through the open window.

And the injury to the embalmed cat's throat? That might have happened when the ancient undertaker, just before sealing up the cat's coffin, stole the jewel that he knew would be there under the wrappings.

Possible? What do you think?

Demon Tree

A lot of people didn't like the tall, powerfully built Dutch civil engineer Jan Bekker, for he was a pretty hard character and he had stepped on a good many toes. But everyone admitted that whatever his faults, Bekker was a determined man who got things done.

It was just before World War II and Bekker was in charge of a construction unit, composed mainly of native labor. He had been hired to build a road along the mountainous west coast of Sumatra between Cota Raja and

Sibolga. There had been the usual snags, but work was going ahead according to plan.

One morning, Bekker received two visitors—the headman and witch doctor of the village—both in a state of agitation. Bekker managed to make out that they wanted him to alter the road's course in order to avoid a grove of tamarind trees, the next target for Bekker's bulldozers. The men said that the trees were taboo—and that the tallest one was the home of a demon named Subarjo, who would bring down a terrible vengeance on anyone who disturbed him.

Bekker had heard some of his men murmuring fearfully and now he gave a loud snort of anger. Facing them, he bellowed: "I fear neither man nor demon. And to prove it, I am going to pull down those trees— starting with the biggest one!"

Unlike the headman, whose face was contorted with fear, the witch doctor showed no emotion. He stared impassively at Bekker for a few seconds, then picked up a stick and drew a line on the earth across the road's intended course.

"Your road will not be built beyond this point," he said calmly, then turned and strode away.

Bekker ordered his men to fasten a chain around the biggest tamarind and attach it to one of the heavy tractors. Slowly, the big machine began to take the strain—

and at that moment there was a loud, vicious crack. Bekker ducked just in time to avoid the broken end of the chain. It went whistling past and smashed the skull of one of the laborers.

At the same instant, a scream of agony rang out. The tractor had veered to one side and crushed a second workman under its tracks.

While the men were being buried, the witch doctor and the headman returned. "Two lives have already been lost because of the wrath of Subarjo," the witch doctor said. "Once again I must ask you to leave his spirit in peace and to turn the road aside."

Bekker's patience snapped. "Now, listen," he shouted, "my job is to build this road—and I'm going to do it on time and as planned, even if I have to uproot every blasted tree in Sumatra!"

Bekker's men were terrified by this time, and it took a great deal to persuade them to return to work. But eventually they went back.

Once again, chains were fastened around the tree and the big tamarind creaked and groaned as the tractors took the strain. An electric, fearful atmosphere hung over the spot as the men watched breathlessly. To them—and to Bekker, too—it seemed as though the tree was fighting back, resisting the pull of the tractor with uncanny strength. But at last it gave a loud groan, as though of despair, and came shuddering up out of the earth. And as it did so, the workmen recoiled in sheer horror.

For there, entwined firmly among the roots, was a human skeleton.

Even Bekker was taken aback—but only for a moment. Striding forward, he surveyed the pitiful bones—and then turned to face his men. "There is your demon—no wonder he could not rest in peace. Look— he is pierced through by the roots. Take these bones and bury them somewhere else in a quiet place where he will no longer be in torment. We start work again on the road in the morning."

When he finished speaking, Bekker noticed that his men seemed relieved. Some of them were even smiling. He turned to see what effect his words had on the witch doctor, but the man was gone.

Bekker had an uneasy feeling, though, that his victory had not been as complete as he might have wished.

Even so, he wasn't prepared for the shock that await- ed him the following morning. At the exact spot where the witch doctor had drawn his line in the dust, the ground was split by a chasm several yards in length and three feet in width. Other smaller cracks radiated out- wards towards the grove of tamarinds. The entire sur- face of the ground was scarred with them. And they were natural—not man-made—as Bekker suspected at first.

How or why the cracks had appeared, literally overnight, was beyond Bekker. He only knew that he could never build his road straight through the tamarind grove now.

The tamarind grove still stands, and the road that Bekker built curves around it in a wide loop that the local inhabitants call Subarjo's Bend. And a few yards from the trees, the bones of Subarjo himself lie still, peaceful and undisturbed, in the spot where Bekker laid them.

The legend of the demon tree has been forgotten.

Partying with
the Ouija Board

It was a frosty February night in 1963, and many of the guests had come to the party in Norfolk, England, from towns as far as 50 or 60 miles away. Four had come a mere 30 miles. These four discovered at 11:30 that night that they had been selected to die.

It was a Ouija that gave the message. All that is needed for a Ouija is a board that shows the letters of the alphabet in a semi-circle, as well as the words "Yes" and "No," and a light wineglass. To work it, the operator positions the glass upside down in the center and touches the base with one finger. Presumably, the spirits of the dead channel enough energy into the glass to move it across the table to spell out messages or answer Yes or No.

The Ouija board had become the fad of the moment. The usual light-hearted questions were asked and the glass rumbled around, giving obedient answers.

Mike Chambers, who had just joined the group, was worried about driving home. Addressing the air above the table, he asked, "What sort of road conditions will there be?"

After a pause, the glass gave a surprisingly clear answer: *Ice patches . . . bend*

This direct message inspired more questions: "How far away?" *Many miles.* "Will there be an accident?" *Yes.* "Will anyone be killed?" *Four people . . . people four.* Then the glass appeared to lose interest and meandered around the board. But the group was fired with a morbid interest.

"What is the nearest landmark to the accident?" *Marsham Arms.*

The Marsham Arms was an inn midway between Norwich and the little fishing town of Sheringham, where the party was being held. Furthermore, it stood on a bend near a crossroads, fulfilling other factors the Ouija had noted.

Two more questions were asked that would set the seal of doom on the four people. The first was "What time is this accident to take place?"

After much wandering and slithering, the glass spelled out *One o'clock.*

Mike Chambers had already decided to get home by 1:30, which meant he had to leave the party by 12:15. He realized that, if he followed this schedule, he would be rounding the bend on which the fateful Marsham Arms stood at just about one o'clock.

Hardly knowing that he was asking the clinching question, he dumbly watched the glass move to *Yes.* His question: "Will anyone in this room be involved?"

Since Mike's car was the only one going in the direction of Norwich, it was obvious to everyone in the room that he and his friends were the ones referred to by the wineglass.

The party had died. As the guests filed out the door, one of them turned and said to the hostess: "Why not keep Mike and the others back a little longer? That way they won't be near the Marsham Arms when the accident is supposed to happen."

It seemed such a good idea that Mike was glad to agree. He started out exactly an hour after he had intended to leave.

During the homeward journey, the prophecy was apparently forgotten. But not for long. Rounding a bend a few miles from Sheringham, Mike's small car skidded wildly. In a shaky voice, one of the girls said, "Phew, ice patches, just like it said."

Heedful of the ice menace, Mike drove more slowly. At last they came to the rise that overlooked the Marsham Arms Inn.

The car radio was playing a pop tune. The road, as they gazed down at the sleeping inn, descended at a shallow angle until, curving left, it ran onto the crossroads. The ice on it glittered in the moonlight.

There had been no accident that night. There were no skid marks, no wrecked cars.

As they entered the wide bend, the music from the radio stopped. An announcer's voice came over the air.

"This is the American Forces Network, Frankfurt," the voice said. "The time is now exactly one o'clock Central European time."

As he spoke, Chambers and his friends saw the headlights of another car flashing past the stark trees that lined the road. The car was moving too fast to round the bend with the ice they *knew* to be on it.

Reg, sitting behind the driver, said it "It really is one o'clock! We forgot, the clock goes back for winter!"

At that time the British still kept up their wartime practice of moving the time backwards or forward an hour in winter and summer. The four realized that one o'clock in Germany was in reality one o'clock in England, not an hour later as their clocks said.

The oncoming car, a Jaguar, roared over the cross-roads directly in their path. Someone shouted, "Brake—for God's sake!"

Mike knew better. "I can't!" he cried. Braking on that treacherous surface would throw the car into an uncontrollable skid. There was only one way to slow down, and it was only slightly less dangerous. Mike double declutched and changed gear from fourth to second. The engine howled, the gears screamed, and the car shuddered as its forward motion was slowed by its own engine going slower than the wheels it drove.

At that moment, the other car hit the ice. Its front slipped around, headlights glaring. The massive hood of the Jaguar swung around and pointed towards them. Swift as a bullet, it slithered across the road, hit the bank mere feet in front of them and bounced clear. Then it bounced again briefly before plunging its gleaming snout once more into the scarred earth.

At that moment, Mike's car crept forward through the gap between the bank and the Jaguar, as the other car bounced off. Mike cleared it, just as the giant sports car lunged forward and hit into the space where Mike's car had been seconds before. Had it hit their flimsy car, they would have been steamrollered. Surely, they all would have been killed!

Those are the facts. The direful prophecy was fulfilled in most ways: There were ice patches and there was certainly one outside the Marsham Arms. There was an accident and it did involve four of the people at the party. It took place at one o'clock. *But no one was killed.* The other driver merely suffered a concussion.

How much had reading the future altered it? If he had not known of the future accident, Mike Chambers would have left at the time he originally intended, not an hour later. But having been alerted, he took a risk with his car that he would not normally have taken. He said later that had it not been for the warning, he would have expected the other driver to slow down in time.

Of course, there is another question, and it is real and ominous. Is it certain that the accident was due to happen on the night of the party? Or might it take place on some frosty night in the future . . . ?

You Will Die at Midnight

Probably the most amazing case ever recorded of a death premonition concerned Thomas, Lord Lyttelton.

The remarkable events took place in November, 1779. Lyttelton had gone from London to his country house in Epsom, where he was convalescing after an illness. Walking in the large conservatory with Lady Affleck and her two daughters, Lyttelton noticed a robin perched on an orange tree close by. He tried to catch it, but failed. Seeing the ladies exchange amused glances, he vowed he would catch it—even if it killed him. After a long chase, he succeeded.

The next morning, Lyttelton appeared at the breakfast table, so pale and haggard that his guests anxiously asked him if anything was the matter. Finally, he told them a strange story.

The previous night, after he had lain awake for some time, he heard what sounded like the tapping of a bird at his window, followed by a gentle fluttering of wings in his room. Puzzled, he raised himself on an elbow and saw an amazing sight. In the center of the room stood a beautiful woman dressed in white, with a small robin perched like a falcon on her wrist. This woman told him to prepare for death as he had only a short time to live. When Lyttelton was able to speak, he asked how long he had. The phantom replied, "Not three days. And you will depart at the hour of 12."

For two days Lyttelton fluctuated between despondency and hysterical gaiety. At dinner on Saturday, the third day, he amazed his guests with his wit and vitality. But afterwards, he lapsed into a gloomy silence, and as the evening wore on, he grew restless. He could not sit still but paced restlessly to and fro, muttering incoherently. Every few minutes he took out his pocket watch, gazed at the time, and wiped beads of sweat from his forehead.

Eventually, when the hands of his watch read half-past 11, he went to his room, without a word of farewell to his guests. He had no idea that not only his own watch but every clock in the house had been put forward half an hour by well-meaning friends!

Sitting up in bed, watch in hand, Lyttelton awaited the fatal hour of midnight. As the minute hand slowly approached 12, he asked to see his valet's watch and found that it showed the same time as his own.

With pounding heart and straining eyes he watched the minute hand draw nearer and nearer midnight. A minute to go—half a minute. Then it pointed to the fatal hour—and nothing happened. It crept slowly past. The crisis was over!

Lyttelton put down the watch with a sigh of relief, then broke into wild, hysterical giggling. He spoke to his valet for ten minutes more and seemed to be his normal self once again, completely at ease.

Then he remembered his nightly dose of medicine and asked his valet to prepare it. As no spoon was at hand, the valet stirred it with the handle of a toothbrush that lay on the bedside table. Lyttelton scolded him for his dirty habits and ordered him to fetch a proper spoon.

When the servant returned a few minutes later, Lyttelton was lying back on his pillow, breathing heavily and with a strange, haunted look in his eyes. The valet ran downstairs to get help. The alarmed guests rushed to his room, but a few moments later, he was dead, the watch clutched in his hand pointing to half-past 12. In reality, he had died on the very stroke of midnight.

Index

349